FOREWO**|**

We wish to thank the club secretaries of the FA_ _... _irst Division Clubs for their assistance in providing the information contained in this guide. We also wish to thank Bob Budd for the cover artwork and Alex Graham for providing the League and Cup Statistics.

We particularly thank Michael Hayes of the FAI for all of his help and cooperation and for allowing us to include the Season's Fixtures in this guide together with other copyrighted information

When using this guide, readers should note that most clubs also extend the child concessionary prices to include Senior Citizens.

Additional copies of this guide can be obtained directly from us at the address shown on the facing page. Alternatively, orders may be placed securely via our web site – www.soccer-books.co.uk

Finally, we would like to wish our readers a happy and safe spectating season.

John Robinson
EDITOR

CONTENTS

THE FOOTBALL ASSOCIATION OF IRELAND (FAI)

Founded
1921

Address
80 Merrion Square, Dublin 2

Phone (01) 703-7500

Fax (01) 661-0931

Eircom FAI Premier Division Clubs for 2005

BOHEMIAN FC

Founded: 1890
Former Names: None
Nickname: 'The Bohs' or 'The Gypsies
Ground: Dalymount Park, Phibsboro, Dublin 7
Record Attendance: 46,700
Pitch Size: 120 × 75 yards

Colours: Red & Black striped shirts with Black shorts
Telephone Nº: (01) 868-0923
Fax Number: (01) 868-6460
Ground Capacity: 6,600
Seating Capacity: 6,600
Web Site: www.bohemians.ie

GENERAL INFORMATION

Car Parking: Street parking only
Coach Parking: Street parking only
Nearest Railway Station: Connolly
Nearest Bus Station: Busaras
Club Shop: At the ground
Opening Times: Matchdays only
Telephone Nº: (01) 868-0923
Correspondence Address: c/o 20 Shandon Park, Phibsborough, Dublin 7

ADMISSION INFO (2005 PRICES)

Adult Seating: € 12.00 – 15.00
Senior Citizen/Junior Seating: € 5.00
Note: Under-16s are admitted free with a paying adult
Programme Price: € 2.50

DISABLED INFORMATION

Wheelchairs: Accommodated
Helpers: Admitted
Prices: Free of charge for both the disabled and helpers
Disabled Toilets: Available in the Jodi Stand
Contact: Bookings are not necessary

Travelling Supporters' Information:
Routes: From the North (M1): Take the M1 (becomes N1) into Dublin through Whitehall. Go into the right hand lane on Drumcondra Road Lower, pass under the railway bridge and turn right at the lights onto Whitworth Road (just before the Royal Canal). At top of Whitworth Road turn left onto Phibsborough Road*, stay in the right hand lane for approximately 250 metres then turn right at the lights at the Phibsboro Shopping Centre onto Connaught Street. Dalymount is immediately to the left; From the North (N2): Take the N2 (which becomes Finglas Road) into Dublin through Finglas, past Glasnevin Cemetery (round tower on the left) after which traffic merges. Stay on the right into Prospect Road, over Cross Guns Bridge (over the Railway and Royal Canal) onto Phibsborough Road, then as from *; From the City Centre: Travel North along O'Connell Street (GPO on the left) then turn left into Parnell Square West onto Granby Row (the National Wax Museum is on the right). Cross the junction with Dorset Street Upper into St. Mary's Place, veer right at Black Church and right into Mountjoy Street. Cross the junction with Blessington Street into Berkeley Street (becomes Berkeley Road with Mater Hospital on the right) then turn left with St. Peter's Church immediately in front into New Cabra Road then immediate right into St. Peter's Road. Dalymount is immediately to the right; From the West (N3): Take the N3 (Navan Road) into Dublin. Keep left at Cabra heading for Philsborough and at the end of New Cabra Road (with St. Peter's Church to the right) turn left into St. Peter's Road for the ground; From the West (N4): Take the N4 into Dublin, joining the N7 at Con Colbert Road. Cross the major junction with the South Circular Road (SCR) into St. John's Road West (N7). The road veers left at Heuston Station to cross the River Liffey, then turn right onto the city's North Quays, heading East. Within 1km Wolfe Tone Quay becomes Ellis Quay then Arran Quay (Church to the left). Take next left onto Church Street into Constitutional Hill and Phibsborough Road. Pass through the major crossroads with the NCR and (after the Shopping Centre on the left) turn left onto Connaught Street for the ground; From the South West: Take the N7 Naas Road into Inchicore then follow directions as from the West (Con Colbert Road onwards).

BRAY WANDERERS FC

Founded: 1942
Former Names: None
Nickname: 'The Seagulls'
Ground: Carlisle Grounds, Bray, Co. Wicklow
Record Attendance: 5,200 (vs Bohemians – 2002)
Pitch Size: 113 × 70 yards

Colours: Green & White shirts with White shorts
Telephone Nº: (01) 282-8214
Fax Number: (01) 282-8684
Ground Capacity: 5,500
Seating Capacity: 2,200
Web Site: www.braywanderers.ie

GENERAL INFORMATION

Car Parking: Street parking and along the seafront
Coach Parking: Along the seafront
Nearest Railway Station: Bray (adjacent)
Nearest Bus Station: Bray (adjacent)
Club Shop: At the ground
Opening Times: Matchdays only
Telephone Nº: (01) 282-8214

ADMISSION INFO (2005 PRICES)

Adult Standing: € 12.00
Adult Seating: € 12.00
Senior Citizen/Junior Standing: € 6.00
Senior Citizen/Junior Seating: € 6.00
Note: Group rates and family specials are also available
Programme Price: € 2.50

DISABLED INFORMATION

Wheelchairs: Accommodated
Helpers: Admitted
Prices: Free of charge for the disabled and helpers
Disabled Toilets: Available
Contact: (01) 282-8214 (Bookings are necessary)

Travelling Supporters' Information:
Routes: Take the N11/M11 to Bray and the ground is by the seafront adjacent to the railway station.

CORK CITY FC

Founded: 1984
Former Names: None
Nickname: 'City'
Ground: Turners Cross Stadium, Curragh Road, Turners Cross, Cork
Record Attendance: 11,000
Pitch Size: 110 × 72 yards

Colours: Green shirts with White trim, Green shorts
Telephone N°: (021) 431-1526
Fax Number: (021) 450-3638
Ground Capacity: 7,500
Seating Capacity: 6,300
Web Site: www.corkcityfc.ie

GENERAL INFORMATION

Car Parking: Street parking only
Coach Parking: Street parking only
Nearest Railway Station: Kent Station, Cork (2 miles)
Nearest Bus Station: Parnell Place (1½ miles)
Club Shop: At the ground
Opening Times: Matchdays only
Telephone N°: None

ADMISSION INFO (2005 PRICES)

Adult Standing: € 10.00
Adult Seating: € 10.00
Senior Citizen/Junior Standing: € 5.00
Senior Citizen/Junior Seating: € 5.00
Programme Price: € 2.50

DISABLED INFORMATION

Wheelchairs: Accommodated
Helpers: Admitted – € 5.00 entrance fee
Prices: € 5.00 for the disabled.
Disabled Toilets: Available
Contact: (021) 432-1958 (Bookings are necessary)

Travelling Supporters' Information:
Routes: From Dublin and the East: Enter the City on Lower Glanmire Road then turn left into Water Street at the railway bridge onto the one-way system following 'City Centre' signs. Travel along the quays cross at the first bridge (Michael Collins) and straight on over the south channel of the river. Pass over the next bridge (De Valera), on through Albert Street taking the first right and then immediate left onto South Link Road. Thereafter pass under the pedestrian bridge and three flyovers before turning left onto South Douglas Road. Go straight on at the mini-roundabout and left at the traffic lights onto Curragh Road. The Stadium is 200m on the right; From the West: Enter on Carrigohane 'Straight' Road then onto Western Road as far as the University gates then turn left into the one-way system passing the 'Grand Central' amusement arcade on the right. Turn right at the Court House then left into Washington Street (across the front of the Court House) then take a immediate left, next right then right again into South Main Street* arriving at the bridge with the traffic lights (Beamish and Crawford Brewery to the right). Cross the bridge turning left at the Kozy Korner pub. Take the central of three routes at the next junction into Evergreen Road (i.e. the left of the steep climb). Go straight on at the next traffic lights and then right at the following set. The Stadium is 200m on the right; From the North: Follow signs for 'Blackpool'. Take the first right after Blackpool Fire Station then immediate left into Gerald Griffin Street. Go straight on at the traffic lights at north Cathedral junction onto Shandon Street then across the bridge at the end taking a sharp right, then first left and left again at the traffic lights into Adelaide Street then right into North Main Street. Go straight on into South Main Street and follow directions as from *.

DERRY CITY FC

Founded: 1928
Former Names: None
Nickname: 'The Candystripes'
Ground: Brandywell Stadium, Lone Moor Lane, Derry BT48 7EG
Record Attendance: Not known
Pitch Size: 111 × 72 yards

Colours: Red & White striped shirts with Black shorts
Phone Nº: (04871) 281333 – (028) 7128-1333 (UK)
Fax Nº: (04871) 281334 – (028) 7128-1334 (UK)
Ground Capacity: 8,500
Seating Capacity: 3,000
Web Site: www.derrycityfc.net

GENERAL INFORMATION
Car Parking: Street parking only
Coach Parking: At the ground
Nearest Railway Station: Waterside (1 mile)
Nearest Bus Station: Waterside (1 mile)
Club Shop: At the ground
Opening Times: Daily from 10.00am to 4.00pm. Also open on matchdays.

ADMISSION INFO (2005 PRICES)
Adult Standing: £10.00
Adult Seating: £10.00
Senior Citizen/Junior Standing: £8.00
Senior Citizen/Junior Seating: £8.00
Programme Price: £1.00

DISABLED INFORMATION
Wheelchairs: Accommodated
Helpers: Admitted
Prices: Normal prices apply for the disabled and helpers
Disabled Toilets: Available
Contact: Bookings are not necessary

Travelling Supporters' Information:
Routes: The Stadium is situated over the Craigavon Bridge in the Brandywell area of the City, just to the south of the Bogside. Cross the Craigavon Bridge and take the Abercorn Road to Bishop Street Without. Pass the College on the right and continue along to the junction with Lone Moor Road. Turn right and the ground is situated on the right-hand side of the road past the Sports Centre.

DROGHEDA UNITED FC

Founded: 1919
Former Names: None
Nickname: 'Drogs' or 'United'
Ground: United Park, Windmill Road, Drogheda, Co. Louth
Record Attendance: 6,000
Pitch Size: 110 × 75 yards

Colours: Claret & Blue shirts with Blue shorts
Telephone N°: (041) 983-0190
Fax Number: (041) 983-0195
Ground Capacity: 6,000
Seating Capacity: 395
Web Site: www.droghedaunited.ie

GENERAL INFORMATION
Car Parking: At the ground
Coach Parking: At the ground
Nearest Railway Station: Drogheda
Nearest Bus Station: Drogheda
Club Shop: At the ground
Opening Times: Monday to Friday 9.00am to 5.00pm and also on match nights.
Telephone N°: (041) 983-0190

ADMISSION INFO (2005 PRICES)
Adult Standing: € 15.00
Adult Seating: € 20.00
Senior Citizen/Junior Standing: € 8.00
Senior Citizen/Junior Seating: € 13.00
Under-12s: € 5.00 (Standing); € 10.00 (Seating)
Programme Price: € 2.00

DISABLED INFORMATION
Wheelchairs: Accommodated
Helpers: Admitted
Prices: Normal prices apply for the disabled and helpers
Disabled Toilets: Available
Contact: (041) 983-0190 (Bookings are necessary)

Travelling Supporters' Information:
Routes: The ground is situated in the north of Drogheda near 'Our Lady of Lourdes International Training Hospital'. Turn off the M1 at the Nissan garage (Boyne Cars) and the ground is situated opposite the hospital.

FINN HARPS FC

Founded: 1954
Former Names: None
Nickname: 'Harps'
Ground: Finn Park, Ballybofey, Co. Donegal
Record Attendance: 8,000
Pitch Size: 120 × 80 yards

Colours: Blue shirts and shorts
Telephone Nº: (074) 913-0070 (Office)
Fax Number: (074) 913-0075
Ground Capacity: 8,000
Seating Capacity: 600
Web Site: www.finnharps.com

GENERAL INFORMATION
Car Parking: At the ground
Coach Parking: Adjacent to the ground
Nearest Railway Station: Sligo (50 miles)
Nearest Bus Station: Ballybofey
Club Shop: At the ground
Opening Times: Matchdays only
Telephone Nº: (074) 913-0070

ADMISSION INFO (2005 PRICES)
Adult Standing: € 10.00
Adult Seating: € 12.00
Senior Citizen/Junior Standing: € 8.00
Senior Citizen/Junior Seating: € 9.00
Under-12s: € 3.00
Programme Price: € 2.00

DISABLED INFORMATION
Wheelchairs: Accommodated
Helpers: Admitted
Prices: Normal prices apply for the disabled and helpers
Disabled Toilets: None
Contact: (074) 913-0070 (Bookings are necessary)

Travelling Supporters' Information:
Routes: Take the N15 from Londonderry into Ballybofey village centre. Turn left at the 'Options' shop into Navenny Street and the ground is on the left hand side.

LONGFORD TOWN FC

Founded: 1924
Former Names: None
Nickname: 'The Town'
Ground: Flancare Park, Strokestown Road, Longford
Record Attendance: 4,000 (during 2004)
Pitch Size: 110 × 72 yards

Colours: Red & Black striped shirts with Black shorts
Telephone Nº: (043) 48983 (Club Secretary)
Fax Number: (090) 649-3311
Ground Capacity: 4,500
Seating Capacity: 4,500
Web Site: www.longfordtownfc.com

GENERAL INFORMATION
Car Parking: At the ground
Coach Parking: At the ground
Nearest Railway Station: Longford (2 miles)
Nearest Bus Station: Longford (2 miles)
Club Shop: None usually except around Christmas time

ADMISSION INFO (2005 PRICES)
Adult Seating: € 15.00
Senior Citizen/Junior Seating: € 10.00
Under-14s: € 5.00 (limited number of spaces available)
Programme Price: Included with the admission charge

DISABLED INFORMATION
Wheelchairs: Accommodated
Helpers: Admitted
Prices: Normal prices apply for the disabled and helpers
Disabled Toilets: Available
Contact: (043) 48983 (Bookings are necessary)

Travelling Supporters' Information:
Routes: From Longford Town Centre: Turn left at the Longford Arms and head towards Castlebar along Strokestown Road. Flancare Park is situated directly off the road about 2 miles outside of Longford.

SHAMROCK ROVERS FC

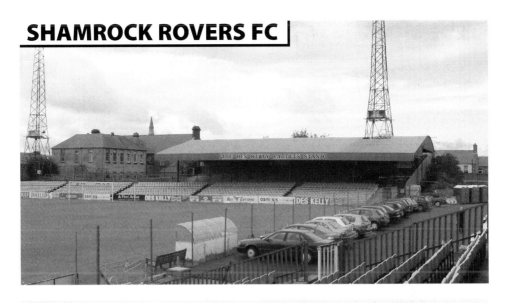

Founded: 1901
Former Names: None
Nickname: 'Rovers' or 'Hoops'
Ground: Dalymount Park, Phibsborough, Dublin 7
Record Attendance: 13,000
Pitch Size: 120 × 75 yards

Colours: Green & White hooped shirts, White shorts
Telephone Nº: (01) 462-2077
Fax Number: (01) 494-0833
Ground Capacity: 6,600 (All seats)
Web Site: www.shamrockrovers.ie
Office: Unit 12A, Tallaght Enterprise Centre, Main Street, Tallaght, Dublin 24

GENERAL INFORMATION
Car Parking: Street parking only
Coach Parking: At the ground
Nearest Railway Station: Connolly
Nearest Bus Station: Busaras
Club Shop: None

ADMISSION INFO (2005 PRICES)
Adult Seating: € 15.00
Senior Citizen/Junior Seating: € 6.00
Programme Price: € 3.00

DISABLED INFORMATION
Wheelchairs: Accommodated
Prices: Normal prices apply for the disabled and helpers
Disabled Toilets: Available in the Jodi Stand
Contact: (01) 462-2077 (Bookings are necessary)

Travelling Supporters' Information:
Routes: From the North (M1): Take the M1 (becomes N1) into Dublin through Whitehall. Go into the right hand lane on Drumcondra Road Lower, pass under the railway bridge and turn right at the lights onto Whitworth Road (just before the Royal Canal). At top of Whitworth Road turn left onto Phibsborough Road*, stay in the right hand lane for approximately 250 metres then turn right at the lights at the Phibsboro Shopping Centre onto Connaught Street. Dalymount is immediately to the left; From the North (N2): Take the N2 (which becomes Finglas Road) into Dublin through Finglas, past Glasnevin Cemetery (round tower on the left) after which traffic merges. Stay on the right into Prospect Road, over Cross Guns Bridge (over the Railway and Royal Canal) onto Phibsborough Road, then as from *; From the City Centre: Travel North along O'Connell Street (GPO on the left) then turn left into Parnell Square West onto Granby Row (the National Wax Museum is on the right). Cross the junction with Dorset Street Upper into St. Mary's Place, veer right at Black Church and right into Mountjoy Street. Cross the junction with Blessington Street into Berkeley Street (becomes Berkeley Road with Mater Hospital on the right) then turn left with St. Peter's Church immediately in front into New Cabra Road then immediate right into St. Peter's Road. Dalymount is immediately to the right; From the West (N3): Take the N3 (Navan Road) into Dublin. Keep left at Cabra heading for Philsborough and at the end of New Cabra Road (with St. Peter's Church to the right) turn left into St. Peter's Road for the ground; From the West (N4): Take the N4 into Dublin, joining the N7 at Con Colbert Road. Cross the major junction with the South Circular Road (SCR) into St. John's Road West (N7). The road veers left at Heuston Station to cross the River Liffey, then turn right onto the city's North Quays, heading East. Within 1km Wolfe Tone Quay becomes Ellis Quay then Arran Quay (Church to the left). Take next left onto Church Street into Constitutional Hill and Phibsborough Road. Pass through the major crossroads with the NCR and (after the Shopping Centre on the left) turn left onto Connaught Street for the ground; From the South West: Take the N7 Naas Road into Inchicore then follow directions as from the West (Con Colbert Road onwards).

SHELBOURNE FC

Founded: 1895
Former Names: None
Nickname: 'Shels'
Ground: Tolka Park, Richmond Road, Drumcondra, Dublin 3
Record Attendance: 9,000 (vs Bohemians)
Pitch Size: 110 × 75 yards

Colours: Red shirts with White shorts
Telephone Nº: (01) 837-5754
Fax Number: (01) 837-5588
Ground Capacity: 9,680
Seating Capacity: 9,680
Web Site: www.shelbournefc.ie

GENERAL INFORMATION
Car Parking: Street parking only
Coach Parking: Street parking only
Nearest Railway Station: Amiens Street (2 miles)
Nearest Bus Stop: Richmond Road, Drumcondra
Club Shop: At the ground
Opening Times: Daily from 10.00am to 4.00pm
Telephone Nº: (01) 837-5754

ADMISSION INFO (2005 PRICES)
Adult Seating: € 15.00
Senior Citizen/Junior Seating: € 10.00
Under-16s: € 6.00 if unaccompanied
Note: Up to 4 children are admitted free per paying adult
Programme Price: Included with the admission charge

DISABLED INFORMATION
Wheelchairs: Accommodated
Helpers: Admitted
Prices: Free of charge for the disabled and helpers
Disabled Toilets: Available
Contact: (01) 837-5536 (Bookings are necessary)

Travelling Supporters' Information:
Routes: From the City Centre: Take the N1 (Belfast) road to Drumcondra and the ground is situated in Richmond Road, adjacent to Holy Cross College over the Drumcondra bridge.

ST. PATRICK'S ATHLETIC FC

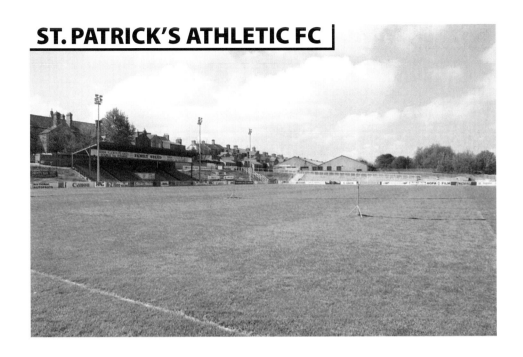

Founded: 1929
Former Names: St. Patrick's FC
Nickname: 'Pats' or 'Dublin Saints'
Ground: Richmond Park, 125 Emmet Road, Dublin 8
Record Attendance: 13,000
Pitch Size: 110 × 72 yards

Colours: Red and White shirts and shorts
Telephone Nº: (01) 454-6332
Fax Number: (01) 454-6211
Ground Capacity: 5,900
Seating Capacity: 2,000
Web Site: www.stpatsfc.com

GENERAL INFORMATION

Car Parking: At the ground
Coach Parking: At the ground
Nearest Railway Station: Richmond Park (1 mile)
Nearest Bus Station: Aston Quay (3 miles)
Club Shop: At the ground
Opening Times: Matchdays only
Telephone Nº: (01) 454-6332

ADMISSION INFO (2005 PRICES)

Adult Standing: € 10.00
Adult Seating: € 15.00
Senior Citizen/Student Standing: € 8.00
Senior Citizen/Student Seating: € 10.00
Junior Standing: € 5.00
Junior Seating: € 7.00
Specials: Family tickets are available
Programme Price: € 2.00

DISABLED INFORMATION

Wheelchairs: Accommodated
Helpers: Admitted and charged Concessionary rates
Prices: Free of charge for the disabled
Disabled Toilets: Available
Contact: (01) 454-6332 (Bookings are necessary)

Travelling Supporters' Information:
Routes: From Outside Dublin: Exit the M50 at Junction 9 and take the N7 (towards the City Centre) to Inchicore. Turn right at the Black Lion pub into Emmet Road and Richmond Park is on the right hand side; From the City Centre: Take Dame Street, Thomas Street and James Street to Inchicore. Then into Kilmainham and Emmet Road and Richmond Park is on the right.

UNIVERSITY COLLEGE DUBLIN FC

Founded: 1895
Former Names: Catholic University FC
Nickname: 'College' and 'Students'
Ground: Belfield Park, UCD Campus, Belfield, Dublin 4
Record Attendance: 3,750
Pitch Size: 115 × 70 yards

Colours: Navy Blue shirts and shorts
Telephone Nº: (01) 716-2142
Fax Number: (01) 269-8099
Ground Capacity: 1,900
Seating Capacity: 800
Web Site: www.ucd.ie/~soccer
Correspondence: Room 203, Sports Centre UCD, Belfield, Dublin 4

GENERAL INFORMATION

Car Parking: On Campus
Coach Parking: On Campus
Nearest Railway Station: Booterstown (½ mile)
Nearest Bus Station: Aston Quay (2 miles)
Club Shop: At the ground
Opening Times: Matchdays only
Telephone Nº: (01) 716-2142

ADMISSION INFO (2005 PRICES)

Adult Standing: € 15.00
Adult Seating: € 15.00
Senior Citizen/Junior Standing: € 6.00
Senior Citizen/Junior Seating: € 6.00
Programme Price: € 3.00

DISABLED INFORMATION

Wheelchairs: Accommodated
Helpers: Admitted
Prices: Normal prices apply for the disabled and helpers
Disabled Toilets: Available
Contact: Diarmuid McNally

Travelling Supporters' Information:
Routes: From the City Centre: Take the N11 (Bray) Road south to Stillorgan and turn right at the University Campus into Foster's Avenue. Turn first right after North Avenue for the ground which is about ¼ mile along on the left behind a stone wall.

WATERFORD UNITED FC

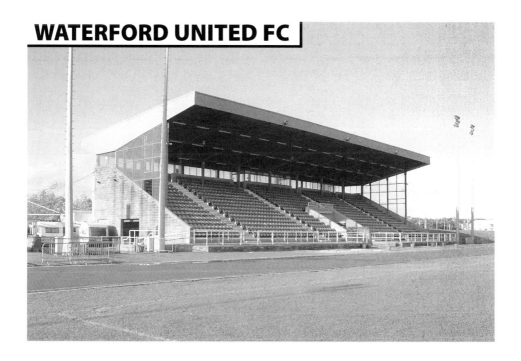

Founded: 1930
Former Names: Waterford FC
Nickname: 'The Blues'
Ground: Waterford Regional Sports Centre, Cork Road, Waterford
Record Attendance: 8,000
Pitch Size: 105 × 75 yards

Colours: Blue shirts and shorts
Telephone Nº: (051) 853222
Fax Number: (051) 853226
Ground Capacity: 8,000
Seating Capacity: 1,250
Web Site: www.waterford-united.ie
E-mail: office@waterford-united.ie

GENERAL INFORMATION

Car Parking: 1,000 spaces available at the Sports Centre
Coach Parking: At the Sports Centre
Nearest Railway Station: Waterford
Nearest Bus Station: Waterford
Club Shop: At the ground
Opening Times: Matchdays only
Telephone Nº: (051) 853222
Correspondence Address: 15 Parnell Street, Waterford

ADMISSION INFO (2005 PRICES)

Adult Standing: € 10.00
Adult Seating: € 15.00
Senior Citizen Standing: € 8.00
Senior Citizen Seating: € 10.00
Under-16s Standing: € 4.00
Under-16s Seating: € 6.00
Programme Price: € 2.50

DISABLED INFORMATION

Wheelchairs: Accommodated
Helpers: Admitted
Prices: Concessionary prices are charge for the disabled and their helpers
Disabled Toilets: Available
Contact: (051) 853222   (Bookings are necessary)

Travelling Supporters' Information:
Routes: Take the N9 to Waterford then, from the train station and bus depot, cross over Rice Bridge. Turn left along the Quay and Parnell Street and go out onto the main Waterford to Cork Road. The ground is situated on the left hand side half a mile out of town a short distance from the Waterford Crystal Factory.

PREMIER DIVISION STATISTICS

Home & Away Score Charts

and

Final League Tables

1995-96

League of Ireland Premier Division 1995-96	Athlone Town AFC	Bohemian FC	Cork City FC	Derry City FC	Drogheda United	Dundalk FC	Galway United FC	St. Patrick's Athletic	Shamrock Rovers	Shelbourne FC	Sligo Rovers FC	University College
Athlone Town AFC (Athlone)		0-3				0-0	1-0	2-2		4-3		
		2-5	2-4	1-1	0-2	0-0	0-2	0-1	2-0	1-2	1-2	1-0
Bohemian FC (Dublin)			1-0	1-1				0-0	1-0		1-2	3-1
	3-1		1-1	1-0	6-0	3-2	3-0	0-1	1-1	1-0	2-0	0-0
Cork City FC (Cork)	0-2				2-1		3-0	0-0		2-1		
	2-0	1-0		0-1	1-2	0-2	1-1	1-0	2-0	1-1	2-1	2-1
Derry City FC (Derry)	1-1		2-1		1-1	0-1					4-0	1-1
	5-3	1-1	2-0		1-0	1-1	2-0	5-1	1-1	1-2	1-2	3-1
Drogheda United FC (Drogheda)	0-1	0-1				2-1	6-1			1-3	0-1	
	0-1	2-5	2-2	2-2		3-2	3-0	1-3	1-2	1-1	0-0	0-1
Dundalk FC (Dundalk)		2-4	0-1				1-2	0-0		0-1		
	2-1	1-2	0-0	2-1	2-2		2-0	3-2	1-0	1-1	0-1	2-0
Galway United FC (Galway)		0-2		0-3	2-1			0-2	1-3			0-2
	2-2	1-5	3-1	1-1	0-3	0-1		0-1	1-1	1-1	2-3	1-1
St. Patrick's Athletic FC (Dublin)				1-1	3-2		3-0		2-2	3-0		2-0
	3-2	3-3	2-1	3-3	1-0	2-1	1-2		1-0	2-1	1-0	2-1
Shamrock Rovers FC (Dublin)	2-1		2-0	2-1	1-0							2-0
	1-1	1-0	1-1	2-0	1-1	1-0	2-1	0-1		0-1	0-2	0-2
Shelbourne FC (Dublin)		1-0		1-0	1-1	0-1		1-2	2-1			
	1-0	1-0	1-1	1-2	0-0	3-1	2-0	1-1	3-0		0-0	1-1
Sligo Rovers FC (Sligo)	2-1		4-1				0-2	1-1	3-1			
	4-2	0-0	3-1	1-1	1-0	3-3	3-2	0-0	0-1	0-1		2-0
University College Dublin AFC (Dublin)	1-2		2-1	4-1	0-0					3-2	3-1	
	3-0	3-1	0-1	2-0	0-0	1-2	2-0	0-2	0-1	0-3	2-1	

	Premier Division	**Pd**	**Wn**	**Dw**	**Ls**	**GF**	**GA**	**Pts**	
1.	ST. PATRICK'S ATHLETIC FC (DUBLIN)	33	19	10	4	53	34	67	
2.	Bohemian FC (Dublin)	33	18	8	7	60	29	62	
3.	Sligo Rovers FC (Sligo)	33	16	7	10	45	38	55	
4.	Shelbourne FC (Dublin)	33	15	9	9	45	33	54	
5.	Shamrock Rovers FC (Dublin)	33	14	8	11	32	32	50	
6.	Derry City FC (Derry)	33	11	13	9	50	38	46	
7.	Dundalk FC (Dundalk)	33	11	9	13	38	39	42	
8.	University College Dublin AFC (Dublin)	33	12	6	15	38	40	42	
9.	Cork City FC (Cork)	33	12	8	13	37	41	41	*
10.	Athlone Town AFC (Athlone)	33	8	7	18	38	59	31	PO
11.	Drogheda United FC (Drogheda)	33	7	9	17	39	51	30	R
12.	Galway United FC (Galway)	33	5	6	22	26	67	21	R
		396	148	100	148	501	501	541	

* Cork City FC (Cork) had 3 points deducted for fielding an ineligible player. The club went into liquidation in January 1996 but were saved from extinction and moved from Bishopstown to Turner's Cross.

1996-97

League of Ireland Premier Division 1996-97	Bohemian FC	Bray Wanderers AFC	Cork City FC	Derry City FC	Dundalk FC	Finn Harps FC	Home Farm-Everton	St. Patrick's Athletic	Shamrock Rovers FC	Shelbourne FC	Sligo Rovers FC	University College
Bohemian FC (Dublin)	■	1-0	0-2	0-0				0-1			0-0	
	■	1-0	1-0	1-1	3-0	3-1	1-1	2-1	1-1	1-1	0-2	1-0
Bray Wanderers AFC (Bray)	0-1	■		2-5	0-1	0-0				1-1		2-0
	1-5	■	0-0	2-3	1-0	0-1	1-0	0-1	3-4	0-4	2-2	0-2
Cork City FC (Cork)	3-1		■			1-0	0-0		1-1	0-1	1-0	
	0-0	3-1	■	0-1	0-0	0-1	2-1	1-1	0-1	3-1	1-2	1-0
Derry City FC (Derry)			0-2	■			1-1	2-0	1-1		0-2	
	1-0	5-1	0-1	■	5-2	3-0	3-1	1-1	1-0	2-2	0-0	5-0
Dundalk FC (Dundalk)			0-4	0-1	■			2-2	1-3		1-1	
	0-2	2-1	0-1	2-4	■	1-1	2-1	1-0	4-1	0-1	2-1	2-2
Finn Harps FC (Ballybofey)	1-2			0-1	0-0	■	3-0		1-2		3-4	
	2-2	0-0	0-1	0-1	5-0	■	3-2	0-1	0-0	3-2	1-1	5-1
Home Farm-Everton FC (Dublin)	2-2	0-1			0-1		■		3-0			2-3
	0-3	1-1	0-2	0-2	0-0	2-3	■	0-2	0-0	0-3	0-0	0-1
St. Patrick's Athletic FC (Dublin)		2-1	0-0		2-1	3-1		■	2-2		4-2	
	5-0	2-2	1-1	1-1	2-2	2-0	1-2	■	0-0	1-1	2-2	1-1
Shamrock Rovers FC (Dublin)	3-1	2-2			2-3				■	6-4		0-0
	3-2	2-0	0-1	1-1	0-2	2-2	2-1	0-1	■	0-2	2-1	1-1
Shelbourne FC (Dublin)	0-1			1-1	0-1	2-0		1-1		■		1-0
	0-1	1-0	3-3	2-2	2-1	1-2	2-0	0-1	2-0	■	3-0	1-0
Sligo Rovers FC (Sligo)		0-1					3-2	1-1	0-3		■	2-0
	2-1	3-2	1-4	0-1	2-1	0-2	0-0	2-0	3-0	1-1	■	2-1
University College Dublin AFC (Dublin)	1-2		3-0	0-1	3-1	0-0		2-0				■
	0-2	2-1	2-1	1-0	1-0	4-0	0-0	0-1	1-0	1-3	1-1	■

Premier Division

	Premier Division	Pd	Wn	Dw	Ls	GF	GA	Pts	
1.	DERRY CITY FC (DERRY)	33	19	10	4	58	27	67	
2.	Bohemian FC (Dublin)	33	16	9	8	43	32	57	
3.	Shelbourne FC (Dublin)	33	15	9	9	52	36	54	
4.	Cork City FC (Cork)	33	15	9	9	38	24	54	
5.	St. Patrick's Athletic FC (Dublin)	33	13	14	6	45	33	53	
6.	Sligo Rovers FC (Sligo)	33	12	11	10	43	43	47	
7.	Shamrock Rovers FC (Dublin)	33	10	13	10	43	46	43	
8.	University College Dublin AFC (Dublin)	33	12	7	14	34	39	43	
9.	Finn Harps FC (Ballybofey)	33	10	9	14	41	43	39	
10.	Dundalk FC (Dundalk)	33	9	9	15	32	50	36	PO
11.	Bray Wanderers AFC (Bray)	33	5	8	29	30	59	23	R
12.	Home Farm-Everton FC (Dublin)	33	3	10	20	26	53	19	R
		396	139	118	139	485	485	535	

League of Ireland Premier Division 1997-98	Bohemian FC	Cork City FC	Derry City FC	Drogheda United	Dundalk FC	Finn Harps FC	Kilkenny City FC	St. Patrick's Ath.	Shamrock Rovers	Shelbourne FC	Sligo Rovers FC	University College
Bohemian FC (Dublin)	■			2-1		1-0	4-3		0-1	0-1		2-0
	■	4-2	1-0	1-1	2-0	4-2	8-1	0-0	1-1	1-0	1-1	0-0
Cork City FC (Cork)	2-0	■	0-1		0-0			1-1				1-2
	1-1	■	2-0	1-1	3-0	3-1	1-0	0-1	2-1	4-4	1-1	1-0
Derry City FC (Derry)	1-0		■	3-0	0-0	0-0				1-2		0-3
	1-0	1-1	■	4-1	1-2	1-0	1-1	1-1	0-1	2-2	0-0	1-1
Drogheda United FC (Drogheda)		1-2		■			1-1	1-2	0-1		1-1	
	0-1	1-2	0-1	■	1-0	0-2	0-0	1-3	1-3	0-1	2-1	0-0
Dundalk FC (Dundalk)	3-3			0-2	■	2-1	1-0			2-1		1-2
	2-2	1-0	0-1	1-1	■	2-0	3-0	0-0	0-0	0-1	5-0	1-1
Finn Harps FC (Ballybofey)		1-2		1-0		■		0-2		0-0		1-2
	3-2	2-1	1-0	2-0	0-1	■	2-1	1-2	2-1	3-1	1-1	1-0
Kilkenny City FC (Kilkenny)		1-2	1-0			2-2	■	1-2	1-1		2-1	
	1-1	0-2	0-5	2-1	1-2	2-3	■	0-2	1-2	1-3	0-1	1-1
St. Patrick's Athletic FC (Dublin)	0-2		1-0	4-2				■	0-0			1-0
	0-0	3-3	0-0	2-0	1-0	1-0	1-0	■	2-0	2-3	1-2	1-1
Shamrock Rovers FC (Dublin)		2-2	3-1		5-2	2-2		0-1	■	0-0		
	2-1	1-3	1-0	0-0	1-2	2-1	1-0	0-1	■	0-2	1-1	2-0
Shelbourne FC (Dublin)		1-1		1-0			3-0		2-1	■	2-0	
	0-1	3-1	1-0	5-0	2-0	3-2	2-1	0-2	1-1	■	3-0	3-1
Sligo Rovers FC (Sligo)	2-1	4-1	1-1		3-0	0-2		1-1			■	
	2-2	0-2	3-0	2-1	3-3	2-2	2-0	3-4	0-1	1-1	■	2-1
University College Dublin AFC (Dublin)				1-1			1-0		0-0	2-3	5-1	■
	2-1	0-0	1-2	3-0	1-3	0-0	1-2	1-1	0-3	2-1	1-1	■

Premier Division

	Premier Division	Pd	Wn	Dw	Ls	GF	GA	Pts	
1.	ST. PATRICK'S ATHLETIC FC (DUBLIN)	33	19	11	3	46	24	68	
2.	Shelbourne FC (Dublin)	33	20	7	6	58	32	67	
3.	Cork City FC (Cork)	33	14	11	8	50	40	53	
4.	Shamrock Rovers FC (Dublin)	33	14	10	9	41	32	52	
5.	Bohemian FC (Dublin)	33	13	11	9	50	36	50	
6.	Dundalk FC (Dundalk)	33	12	9	12	41	43	45	
7.	Sligo Rovers FC (Sligo)	33	10	14	9	46	49	44	
8.	Finn Harps FC (Ballybofey)	33	12	7	14	41	43	43	
9.	Derry City FC (Derry)	33	10	10	13	30	31	40	
10.	University College Dublin AFC (Dublin)	33	9	12	12	36	38	39	PO
11.	Kilkenny City FC (Kilkenny)	33	4	7	22	27	63	19	R
12.	Drogheda United FC (Drogheda)	33	2	9	22	20	55	15	R
		396	139	118	139	486	486	535	

League of Ireland Premier Division 1998-99	Bohemian FC	Bray Wanderers AFC	Cork City FC	Derry City FC	Dundalk FC	Finn Harps FC	St. Patrick's Athletic FC	Shamrock Rovers FC	Shelbourne FC	Sligo Rovers FC	University College Dublin	Waterford AFC
Bohemian FC (Dublin)	■	0-0	0-2		2-1	0-1						0-1
		1-2	0-2	0-1	1-0	2-3	1-1	1-1	2-0	0-1	3-0	0-1
Bray Wanderers AFC (Bray)		■	1-3		1-0					0-1	1-2	0-1
	0-1		0-1	0-1	0-0	0-0	1-4	3-4	1-0	1-1	0-0	6-0
Cork City FC (Cork)			■	0-1	2-0	2-1	--	3-0	2-1			0-4
	0-0	3-0		2-1	4-1	2-0	1-2	3-1	2-1	1-0	1-2	5-0
Derry City FC (Derry)	0-1	1-1		■		1-0	0-0		1-0			
	0-2	5-1	1-1		0-1	2-1	0-1	1-1	0-1	2-0	2-0	1-0
Dundalk FC (Dundalk)				0-1	■			1-1	1-2	3-2	0-2	
	0-1	0-1	1-1	2-2		0-0	2-0	1-1	1-2	0-2	2-0	2-0
Finn Harps FC (Ballybofey)		0-3			1-0	■	0-3	4-1		1-0		2-0
	1-0	6-2	1-1	2-2	0-0		2-1	2-1	3-2	1-1	0-0	1-2
St. Patrick's Athletic FC (Dublin)	1-3	1-0	1-0		1-0		■			4-0	0-0	
	3-0	3-0	2-0	1-0	3-1	2-2		3-0	2-1	4-1	1-0	2-0
Shamrock Rovers FC (Dublin)	1-1	0-0		1-0			0-1	■		0-0		
	3-0	0-1	0-3	0-0	1-1	2-0	2-1		2-1	1-1	2-0	0-0
Shelbourne FC (Dublin)	1-2				2-0	1-1	1-0		■	1-0		0-2
	2-1	1-0	3-3	2-0	1-2	0-0	0-1	2-2		1-1	1-1	1-0
Sligo Rovers FC (Sligo)	2-1		2-5	2-0		2-0		1-0		■		2-1
	2-2	0-0	0-2	3-3	2-0	1-1	1-4	2-3	1-3		0-1	1-1
University College Dublin AFC (Dublin)	2-0	1-3	2-2	2-1					0-1	0-0	■	
	2-0	3-1	0-1	2-2	0-0	3-0	2-2	0-2	1-1	2-0		1-1
Waterford United FC (Waterford)			1-0	2-0		0-0	1-0				1-2	■
	0-0	1-0	0-2	1-2	1-0	0-3	0-2	1-1	0-0	1-1	1-0	

Premier Division

	Premier Division	Pd	Wn	Dw	Ls	GF	GA	Pts	
1.	ST. PATRICK'S ATHLETIC FC (DUBLIN)	33	22	7	4	58	21	73	
2.	Cork City FC (Cork)	33	21	7	5	62	25	70	
3.	Shelbourne FC (Dublin)	33	13	8	12	37	35	47	
4.	Finn Harps FC (Ballybofey)	33	12	10	11	39	40	46	
5.	Derry City FC (Derry)	33	12	9	12	34	32	45	
6.	University College Dublin AFC (Dublin)	33	10	12	11	31	32	42	
7.	Waterford United FC (Waterford)	33	11	9	13	21	37	42	
8.	Shamrock Rovers FC (Dublin)	33	9	13	11	34	40	40	
9.	Sligo Rovers FC (Sligo)	33	9	11	13	37	50	38	
10.	Bohemian FC (Dublin)	33	10	7	16	28	37	37	PO
11.	Bray Wanderers AFC (Bray)	33	8	8	17	30	45	32	R
12.	Dundalk FC (Dundalk)	33	6	9	18	23	40	27	R
		396	143	110	143	434	434	539	

1999-2000

League of Ireland Premier Division 1999-2000	Bohemian FC	Cork City FC	Derry City FC	Drogheda United FC	Finn Harps FC	Galway United FC	St. Patrick's Athletic	Shamrock Rovers	Shelbourne FC	Sligo Rovers FC	University College	Waterford AFC
Bohemian FC (Dublin)	■	0-0					0-1	0-0	1-1	4-1	1-2	
	■	3-0	3-0	2-1	1-0	1-3	0-0	1-3	0-1	3-2	1-0	0-2
Cork City FC (Cork)	2-1	■		3-1			1-1			0-0	1-1	
	1-1	■	0-0	3-0	2-0	3-0	1-0	2-0	1-2	0-1	1-0	0-0
Derry City FC (Derry)		1-4	■	2-1				0-0		0-0	2-0	1-1
	0-0	1-0	■	0-2	2-0	2-0	0-3	1-0	1-0	1-3	0-2	3-0
Drogheda United FC (Drogheda)	0-3			■	0-2		0-3	0-0			0-5	1-0
	0-2	0-0	1-2	■	3-2	3-1	1-2	0-4	0-0	1-1	0-1	1-1
Finn Harps FC (Ballybofey)	0-0	1-1	1-2		■			2-3	2-1			
	0-1	1-2	1-1	0-0	■	1-2	1-1	1-0	0-1	2-1	0-0	4-0
Galway United FC (Galway)	0-1	0-2	2-1	2-2	0-4	■	1-0					
	1-2	1-4	0-2	1-1	1-3	■	1-2	0-3	0-0	5-0	2-1	0-0
St. Patrick's Athletic FC (Dublin)			1-1		1-0		■	0-0	1-2			0-0
	1-3	2-0	1-2	1-0	2-1	3-0	■	1-1	1-1	3-2	0-0	1-0
Shamrock Rovers FC (Dublin)		1-2		3-3	0-0			■	2-1	4-2		1-2
	0-1	1-3	3-0	4-1	3-1	2-1	2-1	■	1-1	4-1	0-0	1-0
Shelbourne FC (Dublin)		4-0	2-2	0-0		1-1			■		2-1	
	1-0	3-2	2-0	1-0	1-1	1-1	1-0	3-0	■	1-0	0-0	1-0
Sligo Rovers FC (Sligo)			0-0			1-1	2-2		0-4	■	0-1	
	0-0	0-5	2-0	1-1	1-1	1-0	0-1	3-5	2-4	■	1-2	1-0
University College Dublin AFC (Dublin)					1-1	1-1	2-1	1-1			■	2-1
	0-2	2-2	1-0	3-0	1-0	0-2	2-2	3-0	0-2	1-1	■	2-2
Waterford United FC (Waterford)	0-0	2-2			1-0	0-0				0-2	1-1	■
	0-2	1-3	2-2	1-0	2-3	1-2	3-1	0-0	0-0	1-0	0-2	■

Premier Division

	Premier Division	Pd	Wn	Dw	Ls	GF	GA	Pts	
1.	SHELBOURNE FC (DUBLIN)	33	19	12	2	49	20	69	
2.	Cork City FC (Cork)	33	16	10	7	53	32	58	
3.	Bohemian FC (Dublin)	33	16	9	8	40	23	57	
4.	University College Dublin AFC (Dublin)	33	13	12	8	40	29	51	
5.	Shamrock Rovers FC (Dublin)	33	13	11	9	49	36	50	
6.	St. Patrick's Athletic FC (Dublin)	33	13	11	9	40	31	50	
7.	Derry City FC (Derry)	33	12	10	11	32	38	46	
8.	Finn Harps FC (Ballybofey)	33	8	10	15	39	41	34	
9.	Galway United FC (Galway)	33	8	10	15	32	49	34	
10.	Waterford United FC (Waterford)	33	7	12	14	24	38	33	PO
11.	Sligo Rovers FC (Sligo)	33	5	10	18	31	60	25	R
12.	Drogheda United FC (Drogheda)	33	4	11	18	21	53	23	R
		396	134	128	134	450	450	530	

2000-2001

League of Ireland Premier Division 2000-2001	Bohemian FC	Bray Wanderers	Cork City FC	Derry City FC	Finn Harps FC	Galway United FC	Kilkenny City FC	Longford Town	St. Patrick's Ath.	Shamrock Rovers	Shelbourne FC	University College
Bohemian FC (Dublin)	■	1-0	0-1		5-1	2-2			2-1			
	■	3-1	1-1	1-1	1-0	5-0	2-1	2-1	2-2	0-1	0-1	2-0
Bray Wanderers AFC (Bray)		■	2-1		2-1	5-0		4-1				1-0
	3-1	■	1-0	1-0	0-0	0-1	3-0	3-1	2-2	2-2	3-0	1-2
Cork City FC (Cork)	1-0		■	1-0		3-1		1-0	0-4			2-2
	0-0	0-0	■	0-2	1-0	2-0	3-1	0-0	1-0	1-2	1-1	2-1
Derry City FC (Derry)	0-2			■	2-0	0-1		0-0	1-1		3-3	
	1-0	1-1	1-1	■	3-1	0-1	1-0	0-1	1-1	2-0	1-1	0-1
Finn Harps FC (Ballybofey)		4-1	1-1		■		2-0	2-1		2-2		
	1-1	1-0	0-1	0-1	■	1-0	1-1	2-2	0-1	0-0	2-2	1-1
Galway United FC (Galway)					1-1	■	2-0		2-2	1-1	0-0	1-2
	0-2	2-2	0-2	1-0	5-2	■	1-2	1-0	1-1	1-0	1-1	1-4
Kilkenny City FC (Kilkenny)	0-5		1-4	0-1			■	1-1		0-4		
	0-0	2-2	0-0	0-2	0-1	0-1	■	0-1	0-2	1-1	0-3	0-1
Longford Town FC (Longford)	1-3	1-3			2-1			■			0-1	2-0
	1-6	0-1	2-1	1-0	4-1	2-2	2-1	■	0-3	2-1	0-1	2-0
St. Patrick's Athletic FC (Dublin)					1-4		3-0	2-1	■	4-1	2-1	
	2-1	1-1	1-1	1-0	2-1	3-0	3-0	2-4	■	0-1	0-2	1-1
Shamrock Rovers FC (Dublin)	4-6	1-2	1-2	2-3				3-1	1-1	■		
	0-0	1-1	4-1	2-0	2-0	0-0	2-1	3-2	1-2	■	1-3	1-1
Shelbourne FC (Dublin)	2-4	3-2	0-1		0-0		3-1			3-1	■	
	4-2	0-1	2-0	0-1	0-1	3-1	1-0	1-1	3-1	2-2	■	3-1
University College Dublin AFC (Dublin)	3-4		1-1	1-1		1-0			2-1	1-2		■
	0-1	1-1	0-0	0-1	3-2	0-1	2-1	0-2	1-1	2-2	0-1	■

	Premier Division	Pd	Wn	Dw	Ls	GF	GA	Pts	
1.	BOHEMIAN FC (DUBLIN)	33	18	8	7	66	35	62	
2.	Shelbourne FC (Dublin)	33	17	9	7	53	37	60	
3.	Cork City FC (Cork)	33	15	11	7	36	29	56	
4.	Bray Wanderers AFC (Bray)	33	15	10	8	52	35	55	
5.	St. Patrick's Athletic FC (Dublin)	33	14	11	8	54	41	53	
6.	Derry City FC (Derry)	33	12	9	12	31	28	45	
7.	Shamrock Rovers FC (Dublin)	33	10	12	11	50	47	42	
8.	Longford Town FC (Longford)	33	12	6	15	40	47	42	
9.	Galway United FC (Galway)	33	10	10	13	34	47	40	
10.	University College Dublin AFC (Dublin)	33	9	10	14	36	44	37	PO
11.	Finn Harps FC (Ballybofey)	33	8	12	13	36	46	36	R
12.	Kilkenny City FC (Kilkenny)	33	1	6	26	14	66	9	R
		396	141	114	141	502	502	537	

2001-2002

League of Ireland Premier Division 2001-2002	Bohemian FC	Bray Wanderers	Cork City FC	Derry City FC	Dundalk FC	Galway United	Longford Town	Monaghan Utd.	St. Patrick's Ath.	Shamrock Rov.	Shelbourne	U.C. Dublin
Bohemian FC (Dublin)	■			1-0			1-0	3-0		1-1	4-0	3-0
		■	2-0	2-2	1-0	1-1	3-0	1-1	3-0	0-2	0-1	4-6	6-0
Bray Wanderers AFC (Bray)	2-2	■	0-2		1-2	4-1			2-1	0-0		
	0-0		2-2	0-0	5-1	2-0	5-1	5-0	0-2	1-1	0-3	1-1
Cork City FC (Cork)	0-3		■		0-0			5-1		0-2	0-1	
	0-1	2-2		1-0	0-1	4-0	2-1	2-0	2-1	2-1	1-0	0-2
Derry City FC (Derry)		1-2	1-0	■				6-1		3-0		1-1
	1-0	3-1	1-0		1-1	2-0	1-1	2-0	3-1	2-0	0-0	1-1
Dundalk FC (Dundalk)	1-1		4-2		■	1-1			0-1		1-2	1-1
	3-1	0-3	1-3	1-0		1-1	1-1	3-0	0-2	0-0	1-1	1-1
Galway United FC (Galway)	1-5	3-5	0-3	2-3		■	0-0					
	1-5	0-2	1-2	0-1	0-1		1-1	8-0	0-4	0-2	0-1	1-0
Longford Town FC (Longford)		0-0	1-0	1-3			■	2-0	1-1	1-5		
	2-0	3-2	4-1	1-0	2-2	1-2		1-1	3-3	1-2	1-0	1-3
Monaghan United FC (Monaghan)		0-3			0-3	1-2		■	0-4		1-0	0-3
	1-1	1-1	2-2	1-2	1-0	0-0	0-2		1-2	2-3	0-1	1-4
St. Patrick's Athletic FC (Dublin)	2-0	2-1	3-2	3-0		3-1			■	1-0		
	1-1	2-0	1-3	1-0	2-0	3-0	3-2	1-1		2-1	3-2	1-2
Shamrock Rovers FC (Dublin)					4-1	3-0		3-2		■	0-2	0-1
	1-0	4-0	1-3	1-1	1-0	3-0	0-0	4-0	0-0		3-0	3-1
Shelbourne FC (Dublin)			0-1		2-0	3-0		2-1			■	0-0
	1-0	2-0	2-1	1-1	4-0	3-0	2-0	3-1	1-1	2-0		0-1
University College Dublin AFC (Dublin)		0-0	1-0			3-1	1-2		0-0			■
	1-1	1-2	1-1	2-2	2-1	1-2	1-0	1-0	0-0	1-3	2-3	

	Premier Division	Pd	Wn	Dw	Ls	GF	GA	Pts	
1.	SHELBOURNE FC (DUBLIN)	33	19	6	8	50	28	63	
2.	Shamrock Rovers FC (Dublin)	33	17	6	10	54	32	57	
3.	St. Patrick's Athletic FC (Dublin)	33	20	8	5	59	29	53	*
4.	Bohemian FC (Dublin)	33	14	10	9	57	32	52	
5.	Derry City FC (Derry)	33	14	9	10	42	30	51	
6.	Cork City FC (Cork)	33	14	7	12	48	39	49	
7.	University College Dublin AFC (Dublin)	33	12	12	9	40	39	48	
8.	Bray Wanderers AFC (Bray)	33	12	10	11	54	45	46	
9.	Longford Town FC (Longford)	33	10	10	13	41	51	40	PO
10.	Dundalk FC (Dundalk)	33	9	12	12	37	46	39	R
11.	Galway United FC (Galway)	33	5	4	24	28	73	19	R
12.	Monaghan United FC (Monaghan)	33	2	6	25	19	85	12	R
		396	148	100	148	529	529	529	

* St. Patrick's Athletic FC (Dublin) had 9 points deducted for fielding Paul Marney in the first 3 games of the season. This was later revoked after arbitration, however Shelbourne FC appealed against this decision which was taken to the High Court where the appeal was rejected. It was then discovered by the Shelbourne chief executive that Ugandan player Charles Mbabazi Livingstone had not been properly registered by St. Patrick's Athletic for the first 5 games of the season and so St. Patrick's Athletic FC had 15 points deducted.

2002-2003

League of Ireland Premier Division 2002-2003	Bohemian FC	Bray Wanderers	Cork City FC	Derry City FC	Drogheda United	Longford Town	St. Patrick's Ath.	Shamrock Rovers	Shelbourne FC	University College
Bohemian FC (Dublin)	■		2-0	2-2	1-1			3-2		1-1
	■	4-0	1-1	3-2	3-1	1-0	1-1	3-2	1-2	2-1
Bray Wanderers AFC (Bray)	1-3	■		1-2	0-2	2-0			1-2	
	1-1	■	2-3	3-3	3-2	2-2	0-0	1-1	1-5	0-0
Cork City FC (Cork)		3-1	■	2-1			1-1	2-1	0-1	
	1-1	3-0	■	3-1	1-0	1-1	2-0	3-2	3-0	3-2
Derry City FC (Derry)				■		1-1	2-0	0-0	0-1	
	0-3	3-1	0-0	■	2-1	1-1	2-0	1-2	1-0	1-0
Drogheda United FC (Drogheda)			0-0	3-1	■		0-0	0-2		0-1
	0-2	2-1	1-0	2-1	■	0-1	1-2	3-2	0-3	1-0
Longford Town FC (Longford)	1-0		1-0		0-0	■				0-2
	1-2	1-0	3-2	1-1	2-1	■	0-1	0-0	0-2	1-1
St. Patrick's Athletic FC (Dublin)	2-0	1-4	1-0		0-2		■			
	1-1	1-2	4-1	1-0	1-1	2-2	■	1-2	2-2	2-2
Shamrock Rovers FC (Dublin)		3-1				3-2	2-1	■	0-1	0-1
	1-1	2-1	4-1	3-1	5-0	0-1	0-1	■	0-0	0-0
Shelbourne FC (Dublin)	0-1			0-1	1-1	2-0			■	
	1-2	3-1	2-1	2-0	3-3	3-0	1-2	0-1	■	2-1
University College Dublin AFC (Dublin)		0-0	1-0			0-0		0-2		■
	1-2	1-1	1-0	0-2	3-0	0-0	1-0	1-2	1-3	■

	Premier Division	Pd	Wn	Dw	Ls	GF	GA	Pts	
1.	BOHEMIAN FC (DUBLIN)	27	15	9	3	47	27	54	
2.	Shelbourne FC (Dublin)	27	15	4	8	44	26	49	
3.	Shamrock Rovers FC (Dublin)	27	12	7	8	42	29	43	
4.	Cork City FC (Cork)	27	11	6	10	37	34	39	
5.	Longford Town FC (Longford)	27	8	11	8	25	29	35	
6.	University College Dublin AFC (Dublin)	27	8	9	10	23	25	33	
7.	St. Patrick's Athletic FC (Dublin)	27	8	9	10	27	33	33	
8.	Derry City FC (Derry)	27	8	7	12	31	37	31	
9.	Drogheda United FC (Drogheda)	27	8	6	13	26	40	30	PO
10.	Bray Wanderers AFC (Bray)	27	4	8	15	31	53	20	R
		270	97	76	97	333	333	367	

2003

League of Ireland Premier Division 2003	Bohemian FC	Cork City FC	Derry City FC	Drogheda United FC	Longford Town FC	St. Patrick's Athletic FC	Shamrock Rovers FC	Shelbourne FC	University College Dublin	Waterford AFC
Bohemian FC (Dublin)		1-0	3-1	1-1	1-1	3-0	2-1	0-1	2-1	1-1
		1-1	1-1	1-0	1-1	1-2	1-1	1-0	1-0	5-1
Cork City FC (Cork)	1-2		1-0	1-0	0-0	0-2	2-2	1-1	0-0	2-2
	3-2		1-1	4-0	4-1	0-0	1-0	0-0	1-0	1-1
Derry City FC (Derry)	0-3	1-1		0-0	1-1	1-1	1-1	0-0	0-2	1-2
	0-3	1-0		0-1	2-3	2-2	1-1	2-0	1-0	4-1
Drogheda United FC (Drogheda)	2-0	0-1	1-1		0-5	2-2	0-1	0-1	0-0	3-0
	1-2	3-1	1-0		2-2	4-2	1-2	1-1	2-0	1-3
Longford Town FC (Longford)	2-4	0-1	0-1	0-2		2-0	1-2	2-1	2-1	0-1
	1-1	0-3	4-0	0-0		1-1	0-0	0-2	2-1	1-0
St. Patrick's Athletic FC (Dublin)	2-4	0-2	2-2	3-3	1-2		1-0	0-1	0-0	1-0
	1-0	1-1	4-1	3-1	1-1		1-1	0-0	2-0	4-1
Shamrock Rovers FC (Dublin)	0-0	0-2	1-1	3-2	0-1	3-5		1-1	2-0	1-1
	1-2	2-1	5-1	0-0	2-3	1-0		2-4	1-0	0-1
Shelbourne FC (Dublin)	1-3	2-0	3-1	2-0	2-1	2-0	0-2		0-0	3-1
	2-2	1-1	1-0	3-0	3-2	2-2	1-0		1-1	1-1
University College Dublin (Dublin)	0-1	1-1	2-0	2-1	2-0	0-0	1-1	0-1		3-0
	2-1	0-3	1-1	1-0	0-3	0-0	2-2	0-2		1-2
Waterford United FC (Waterford)	2-1	3-0	0-1	0-2	0-0	0-0	3-3	1-2	2-2	
	1-3	2-1	1-1	2-1	1-1	4-2	2-0	0-4	1-1	

	Premier Division	**Pd**	**Wn**	**Dw**	**Ls**	**GF**	**GA**	**Pts**	
1.	SHELBOURNE FC (DUBLIN)	36	19	12	5	52	28	69	
2.	Bohemian FC (Dublin)	36	18	10	8	58	37	64	
3.	Cork City FC (Cork)	36	13	14	9	43	33	53	
4.	Longford Town FC (Longford)	36	12	12	12	46	44	48	
5.	St. Patrick's Athletic FC (Dublin)	36	10	16	10	48	48	46	
6.	Waterford United FC (Waterford)	36	11	12	13	44	58	45	
7.	Shamrock Rovers FC (Dublin)	36	10	14	12	45	46	44	
8.	Drogheda United FC (Drogheda)	36	9	10	17	38	50	37	
9.	Derry City FC (Derry)	36	7	15	14	33	51	36	PO
10.	University College Dublin AFC (Dublin)	36	7	13	16	27	39	34	R
		360	116	128	116	434	434	476	

2004

League of Ireland Premier Division 2004	Bohemian FC	Cork City FC	Derry City FC	Drogheda United FC	Dublin City FC	Longford Town FC	St.Patrick's Athletic	Shamrock Rovers FC	Shelbourne FC	Waterford United FC
Bohemian FC (Dublin)		1-0	0-1	0-0	4-0	1-1	2-2	3-2	2-0	2-2
		2-3	3-0	0-1	2-4	0-0	3-1	2-2	1-1	2-2
Cork City FC (Cork)	1-1		1-1	3-2	1-1	2-0	3-0	1-0	0-1	2-0
	0-1		2-1	0-0	3-1	1-0	2-1	1-1	0-2	2-3
Derry City FC (Derry)	0-0	0-1		1-0	2-3	0-0	1-1	1-0	0-0	1-0
	0-0	1-1		0-2	2-1	0-0	0-0	1-0	0-2	0-1
Drogheda United FC (Drogheda)	0-3	1-3	4-0		2-1	0-1	0-2	3-0	2-5	1-2
	0-3	2-0	2-0		2-0	0-1	0-1	1-0	2-2	0-0
Dublin City FC (Dublin)	0-0	0-1	0-2	2-3		2-1	1-2	1-2	2-3	1-3
	2-1	0-1	0-2	1-1		0-1	1-1	0-4	1-3	3-1
Longford Town FC (Longford)	0-1	1-2	3-0	3-1	2-0		2-1	1-1	4-1	1-1
	0-2	1-1	1-0	0-0	0-0		1-3	1-0	0-2	0-2
St. Patrick's Athletic FC (Dublin)	1-2	0-3	0-1	1-1	2-2	1-0		2-0	0-0	2-1
	0-2	0-2	1-1	0-2	3-1	1-1		1-2	1-2	0-1
Shamrock Rovers FC (Dublin)	0-1	1-1	0-0	1-2	1-3	2-0	3-1		1-4	1-2
	2-1	2-1	1-0	1-2	0-0	1-1	1-2		3-0	4-0
Shelbourne FC (Dublin)	1-1	0-0	0-2	0-2	4-1	3-1	3-1	1-1		2-1
	0-0	2-2	1-0	3-0	2-1	1-1	2-0	1-0		1-0
Waterford United FC (Waterford)	1-1	1-4	1-0	1-3	3-2	0-1	0-2	2-0	3-1	
	0-1	1-1	0-2	2-1	2-1	1-1	0-1	3-1	1-1	

	Premier Division	**Pd**	**Wn**	**Dw**	**Ls**	**GF**	**GA**	**Pts**	
1.	SHELBOURNE FC (DUBLIN)	36	19	11	6	57	37	68	
2.	Cork City FC (Cork)	36	18	11	7	52	32	65	
3.	Bohemian FC (Dublin)	36	15	15	6	51	30	60	
4.	Drogheda United FC (Drogheda)	36	15	7	14	45	43	52	
5.	Waterford United FC (Waterford)	36	14	8	14	44	49	50	
6.	Longford Town FC (Longford)	36	11	13	12	32	34	46	
7.	Derry City FC (Derry)	36	11	11	14	23	32	44	
8.	St. Patrick's Athletic FC (Dublin)	36	11	9	16	38	49	42	
9.	Shamrock Rovers FC (Dublin)	36	10	8	18	41	47	38	
10.	Dublin City FC (Dublin)	36	6	7	23	39	69	25	R
		360	130	100	130	422	422	490	

Note: Derry City 0-1 Waterford United on 18/09/04 was abandoned after 19 minutes due to a floodlight failure. The match was replayed on 02/11/04 with the result 1-0.

The Premier Division was extended to 12 clubs for next season

EIRCOM LEAGUE PREMIER DIVISION FIXTURES 2005

SERIES Nº 1

Friday 18th March	Bohemians vs Shamrock Rovers at Dalymount Park	7.45pm
Friday 18th March	Bray Wanderers vs St. Patrick's Athletic at Carlisle Grounds	7.45pm
Friday 18th March	Drogheda United vs Derry City at United Park	7.45pm
Friday 18th March	Shelbourne vs U.C. Dublin at Tolka Park	8.00pm
Saturday 19th March	Longford Town vs Waterford United at Flancare Park	7.30pm
Saturday 19th March	Finn Harps vs Cork City at Finn Park	7.45pm

SERIES Nº 2

Friday 25th March	Waterford United vs Finn Harps at R.S.C.	7.30pm
Friday 25th March	Cork City vs Bray Wanderers at Turner's Cross	7.45pm
Friday 25th March	Derry City vs Longford Town at Brandywell Stadium	7.45pm
Friday 25th March	St. Patrick's Athletic vs Bohemians at Richmond Park	7.45pm
Friday 25th March	Shamrock Rovers vs Shelbourne at Dalymount Park	7.45pm
Friday 25th March	U.C. Dublin vs Drogheda United at Belfield Park	7.45pm

SERIES Nº 3

Friday 1st April	Bohemians vs Derry City at Dalymount Park	7.45pm
Friday 1st April	Bray Wanderers vs U.C. Dublin at Carlisle Grounds	7.45pm
Friday 1st April	Drogheda United vs St. Patrick's Athletic at United Park	7.45pm
Friday 1st April	Shelbourne vs Waterford United at Tolka Park	8.00pm
Saturday 2nd April	Longford Town vs Cork City at Flancare Park	7.30pm
Saturday 2nd April	Finn Harps vs Shamrock Rovers at Finn Park	7.45pm

SERIES Nº 4

Friday 8th April	Waterford United vs Bohemians at R.S.C.	7.30pm
Friday 8th April	Cork City vs U.C. Dublin at Turner's Cross	7.45pm
Friday 8th April	Bray Wanderers vs Drogheda United at Carlisle Grounds	7.45pm
Friday 8th April	Derry City vs Shelbourne at Brandywell Stadium	7.45pm
Friday 8th April	St. Patrick's Athletic vs Finn Harps at Richmond Park	7.45pm
Friday 8th April	Shamrock Rovers vs Longford Town at Dalymount Park	7.45pm

SERIES Nº 5

Friday 15th April	Bohemians vs Cork City at Dalymount Park	7.45pm
Friday 15th April	Drogheda United vs Shamrock Rovers at United Park	7.45pm
Friday 15th April	U.C. Dublin vs Waterford United at Belfield Park	7.45pm
Friday 15th April	Shelbourne vs St. Patrick's Athletic at Tolka Park	8.00pm
Saturday 16th April	Longford Town vs Bray Wanderers at Flancare Park	7.30pm
Saturday 16th April	Finn Harps vs Derry City at Finn Park	7.45pm

SERIES Nº 6

Friday 22nd April	Bohemians vs Finn Harps at Dalymount Park	7.45pm
Friday 22nd April	Bray Wanderers vs Waterford United at Carlisle Grounds	7.45pm
Friday 22nd April	Cork City vs Drogheda United at Turner's Cross	7.45pm
Friday 22nd April	Derry City vs Shamrock Rovers at Brandywell Stadium	7.45pm
Friday 22nd April	St. Patrick's Athletic vs U.C. Dublin at Richmond Park	7.45pm
Saturday 23rd April	Longford Town vs Shelbourne at Flancare Park	7.30pm

SERIES Nº 7

Friday 29th April	Waterford United vs St. Patrick's Athletic at R.S.C.	7.30pm
Friday 29th April	Drogheda United vs Bohemians at United Park	7.45pm
Friday 29th May	Shamrock Rovers vs Cork City at Dalymount Park	7.45pm
Friday 29th April	U.C. Dublin vs Derry City at Belfield Park	7.45pm
Friday 29th April	Shelbourne vs Bray Wanderers at Tolka Park	8.00pm
Saturday 30th April	Finn Harps vs Longford Town at Finn Park	7.45pm

SERIES Nº 8

Friday 6th May	Cork City vs St. Patrick's Athletic at Turner's Cross	7.45pm
Friday 6th May	Derry City vs Waterford United at Brandywell Stadium	7.45pm
Friday 6th May	Shamrock Rovers vs Bray Wanderers at Dalymount Park	7.45pm
Friday 6th May	U.C. Dublin vs Bohemians at Belfield Park	7.45pm
Friday 6th May	Shelbourne vs Finn Harps at Tolka Park	8.00pm
Saturday 7th May	Longford Town vs Drogheda United at Flancare Park	7.30pm

SERIES Nº 9

Friday 13th May	Waterford United vs Cork City at R.S.C.	7.30pm
Friday 13th May	Bohemians vs Longford Town at Dalymount Park	7.45pm
Friday 13th May	Bray Wanderers vs Derry City at Carlisle Grounds	7.45pm
Friday 13th May	Drogheda United vs Shelbourne at United Park	7.45pm
Friday 13th May	St. Patrick's Athletic vs Shamrock Rovers at Richmond Park	7.45pm
Saturday 14th May	Finn Harps vs U.C. Dublin at Finn Park	7.45pm

SERIES Nº 10

Friday 20th May	Bray Wanderers vs Bohemians at Carlisle Grounds	7.45pm
Friday 20th May	Derry City vs St. Patrick's Athletic at Brandywell Stadium	7.45pm
Friday 20th May	Drogheda United vs Finn Harps at United Park	7.45pm
Friday 20th May	Shamrock Rovers vs Waterford United at Dalymount Park	7.45pm
Friday 20th May	Shelbourne vs Cork City at Tolka Park	8.00pm
Saturday 21st May	Longford Town vs U.C. Dublin at Flancare Park	7.30pm

SERIES Nº 11

Friday 27th May	Waterford United vs Drogheda United at R.S.C.	7.30pm
Friday 27th May	Bohemians vs Shelbourne at Dalymount Park	7.45pm
Friday 27th May	Cork City vs Derry City at Turner's Cross	7.45pm
Friday 27th May	St. Patrick's Athletic vs Longford Town at Richmond Park	7.45pm
Friday 27th May	U.C. Dublin vs Shamrock Rovers at Belfield Park	7.45pm
Saturday 28th May	Finn Harps vs Bray Wanderers at Finn Park	7.45pm

SERIES Nº 12

Friday 3rd June	Waterford United vs Longford Town at R.S.C.	7.30pm
Friday 3rd June	Cork City vs Finn Harps at Turner's Cross	7.45pm
Friday 3rd June	Derry City vs Drogheda United at Brandywell Stadium	7.45pm
Friday 3rd June	St. Patrick's Athletic vs Bray Wanderers at Richmond Park	7.45pm
Friday 3rd June	Shamrock Rovers vs Bohemians at Dalymount Park	7.45pm
Friday 3rd June	U.C. Dublin vs Shelbourne at Belfield Park	7.45pm

WEEKEND ENDING SUNDAY 12th JUNE — FAI CUP SECOND ROUND

SERIES N⁰ 13

Friday 17th June	Bohemians vs St. Patrick's Athletic at Dalymount Park	7.45pm
Friday 17th June	Bray Wanderers vs Cork City at Carlisle Grounds	7.45pm
Friday 17th June	Drogheda United vs U.C. Dublin at United Park	7.45pm
Friday 17th June	Shelbourne vs Shamrock Rovers at Tolka Park	8.00pm
Saturday 18th June	Longford Town vs Derry City at Flancare Park	7.30pm
Saturday 18th June	Finn Harps vs Waterford United at Finn Park	7.45pm

SERIES N⁰ 14

Friday 24th June	Waterford United vs Shelbourne at R.S.C.	7.30pm
Friday 24th June	Cork City vs Longford Town at Turner's Cross	7.45pm
Friday 24th June	Derry City vs Bohemians at Brandywell Stadium	7.45pm
Friday 24th June	St. Patrick's Athletic vs Drogheda United at Richmond Park	7.45pm
Friday 24th June	Shamrock Rovers vs Finn Harps at Dalymount Park	7.45pm
Friday 24th June	U.C. Dublin vs Bray Wanderers at Belfield Park	7.45pm

SERIES N⁰ 15

Friday 1st July	Bohemians vs Waterford United at Dalymount Park	7.45pm
Friday 1st July	Drogheda United vs Bray Wanderers at United Park	7.45pm
Friday 1st July	U.C. Dublin vs Cork City at Belfield Park	7.45pm
Friday 1st July	Shelbourne vs Derry City at Tolka Park	8.00pm
Saturday 2nd July	Longford Town vs Shamrock Rovers at Flancare Park	7.30pm
Saturday 2nd July	Finn Harps vs St. Patrick's Athletic at Finn Park	7.45pm

SERIES N⁰ 16

Friday 8th July	Waterford United vs U.C. Dublin at R.S.C.	7.30pm
Friday 8th July	Bray Wanderers vs Longford Town at Carlisle Grounds	7.45pm
Friday 8th July	Cork City vs Bohemians at Turner's Cross	7.45pm
Friday 8th July	Derry City vs Finn Harps at Brandywell Stadium	7.45pm
Friday 8th July	St. Patrick's Athletic vs Shelbourne at Richmond Park	7.45pm
Friday 8th July	Shamrock Rovers vs Drogheda United at Dalymount Park	7.45pm

SERIES N⁰ 17

Friday 15th July	Waterford United vs Bray Wanderers at R.S.C.	7.30pm
Friday 15th July	Drogheda United vs Cork City at United Park	7.45pm
Friday 15th July	Shamrock Rovers vs Derry City at Dalymount Park	7.45pm
Friday 15th July	U.C. Dublin vs St. Patrick's Athletic at Belfield Park	7.45pm
Friday 15th July	Shelbourne vs Longford Town at Tolka Park	8.00pm
Saturday 16th July	Finn Harps vs Bohemians at Finn Park	7.45pm

SERIES N⁰ 18

Friday 22nd July	Bohemians vs Drogheda United at Dalymount Park	7.45pm
Friday 22nd July	Bray Wanderers vs Shelbourne at Carlisle Grounds	7.45pm
Friday 22nd July	Cork City vs Shamrock Rovers at Turner's Cross	7.45pm
Friday 22nd July	Derry City vs U.C. Dublin at Brandywell Stadium	7.45pm
Friday 22nd July	St. Patrick's Athletic vs Waterford United at Richmond Park	7.45pm
Saturday 23rd July	Longford Town vs Finn Harps at Flancare Park	7.30pm

SERIES Nº 19

Friday 29th July	Waterford United vs Derry City at R.S.C.	7.30pm
Friday 29th July	Bohemians vs U.C. Dublin at Dalymount Park	7.45pm
Friday 29th July	Bray Wanderers vs Shamrock Rovers at Carlisle Grounds	7.45pm
Friday 29th July	Drogheda United vs Longford Town at United Park	7.45pm
Friday 29th July	St. Patrick's Athletic vs Cork City at Richmond Park	7.45pm
Saturday 30th July	Finn Harps vs Shelbourne at Finn Park	7.45pm

SERIES Nº 20

Friday 5th August	Cork City vs Waterford United at Turner's Cross	7.45pm
Friday 5th August	Derry City vs Bray Wanderers at Brandywell Stadium	7.45pm
Friday 5th August	Shamrock Rovers vs St. Patrick's Athletic at Dalymount Park	7.45pm
Friday 5th August	U.C. Dublin vs Finn Harps at Belfield Park	7.45pm
Friday 5th August	Shelbourne vs Drogheda United at Tolka Park	8.00pm
Saturday 6th August	Longford Town vs Bohemians at Flancare Park	7.30pm

SERIES Nº 21

Friday 12th August	Waterford United vs Shamrock Rovers at R.S.C.	7.30pm
Friday 12th August	Bohemians vs Bray Wanderers at Dalymount Park	7.45pm
Friday 12th August	Cork City vs Shelbourne at Turner's Cross	7.45pm
Friday 12th August	St. Patrick's Athletic vs Derry City at Richmond Park	7.45pm
Friday 12th August	U.C. Dublin vs Longford Town at Belfield Park	7.45pm
Saturday 13th August	Finn Harps vs Drogheda United at Finn Park	7.45pm

SERIES Nº 22

Friday 19th August	Bray Wanderers vs Finn Harps at Carlisle Grounds	7.45pm
Friday 19th August	Derry City vs Cork City at Brandywell Stadium	7.45pm
Friday 19th August	Drogheda United vs Waterford United at United Park	7.45pm
Friday 19th August	Shamrock Rovers vs U.C. Dublin at Dalymount Park	7.45pm
Friday 19th August	Shelbourne vs Bohemians at Tolka Park	8.00pm
Saturday 20th August	Longford Town vs St. Patrick's Athletic at Flancare Park	7.30pm

WEEKEND ENDING SUNDAY 28th AUGUST — FAI CUP THIRD ROUND

SERIES Nº 23

Friday 2nd September	Bohemians vs Shamrock Rovers at Dalymount Park	7.45pm
Friday 2nd September	Bray Wanderers vs St. Patrick's Athletic at Carlisle Grounds	7.45pm
Friday 2nd September	Drogheda United vs Derry City at United Park	7.45pm
Friday 2nd September	Shelbourne vs U.C. Dublin at Tolka Park	8.00pm
Saturday 3rd September	Longford Town vs Waterford United at Flancare Park	7.30pm

SERIES Nº 26

Friday 30th September	Waterford United vs Bohemians at R.S.C.	7.30pm
Friday 30th September	Bray Wanderers vs Drogheda United at Carlisle Grounds	7.45pm
Friday 30th September	Cork City vs U.C. Dublin at Turner's Cross	7.45pm
Friday 30th September	Derry City vs Shelbourne at Brandywell Stadium	7.45pm
Friday 30th September	St. Patrick's Athletic vs Finn Harps at Richmond Park	7.45pm
Friday 30th September	Shamrock Rovers vs Longford Town at Dalymount Park	7.45pm

SERIES Nº 27

Friday 7th October	Bohemians vs Cork City at Dalymount Park	7.45pm
Friday 7th October	Drogheda United vs Shamrock Rovers at United Park	7.45pm
Friday 7th October	U.C. Dublin vs Waterford United at Belfield Park	7.45pm
Friday 7th October	Shelbourne vs St. Patrick's Athletic at Tolka Park 8.00pm	
Saturday 8th October	Longford Town vs Bray Wanderers at Flancare Park	7.30pm
Saturday 8th October	Finn Harps vs Derry City at Finn Park	7.45pm

SERIES Nº 28

Friday 14th October	Bohemians vs Finn Harps at Dalymount Park	7.45pm
Friday 14th October	Bray Wanderers vs Waterford United at Carlisle Grounds	7.45pm
Friday 14th October	Cork City vs Drogheda United at Turner's Cross	7.45pm
Friday 14th October	Derry City vs Shamrock Rovers at Brandywell Stadium	7.45pm
Friday 14th October	St. Patrick's Athletic vs U.C. Dublin at Richmond Park	7.45pm
Saturday 15th October	Longford Town vs Shelbourne at Flancare Park	7.30pm

SERIES Nº 29 AND FAI CUP SEMI-FINALS

Friday 21st October	Waterford United vs St. Patrick's Athletic at R.S.C.	7.30pm
Friday 21st October	Drogheda United vs Bohemians at United Park	7.45pm
Friday 21st October	Shamrock Rovers vs Cork City at Dalymount Park	7.45pm
Friday 21st October	U.C. Dublin vs Derry City at Belfield Park	7.45pm
Friday 21st October	Shelbourne vs Bray Wanderers at Tolka Park 8.00pm	
Saturday 22nd October	Finn Harps vs Longford Town at Finn Park	7.45pm

SERIES Nº 30

Friday 28th October	U.C. Dublin vs Bohemians at Belfield Park	7.45pm
Friday 28th October	Cork City vs St. Patrick's Athletic at Turner's Cross	7.45pm
Friday 28th October	Shamrock Rovers vs Bray Wanderers at Dalymount Park	7.45pm
Friday 28th October	Shelbourne vs Finn Harps at Tolka Park	8.00pm
Saturday 29th October	Longford Town vs Drogheda United at Flancare Park	7.30pm
Saturday 29th October	Derry City vs Waterford United at Brandywell Stadium	7.30pm

SERIES Nº 31

Friday 4th November	Waterford United vs Cork City at R.S.C.	7.30pm
Friday 4th November	Bohemians vs Longford Town at Dalymount Park	7.45pm
Friday 4th Novwmber	Bray Wanderers vs Derry City at Carlisle Grounds	7.45pm
Friday 4th November	Drogheda United vs Shelbourne at United Park	7.45pm
Friday 4th November	St. Patrick's Athletic vs Shamrock Rovers at Richmond Park	7.45pm
Saturday 5th November	Finn Harps vs U.C. Dublin at Finn Park	7.45pm

SERIES Nº 32

Friday 11th November	Bray Wanderers vs Bohemians at Carlisle Grounds	7.45pm
Friday 11th November	Derry City vs St. Patrick's Athletic at Brandywell Stadium	7.45pm
Friday 11th November	Drogheda United vs Finn Harps at United Park	7.45pm
Friday 11th November	Shamrock Rovers vs Waterford United at Dalymount Park	7.45pm
Friday 11th November	Shelbourne vs Cork City at Tolka Park	8.00pm
Saturday 12th November	Longford Town vs U.C. Dublin at Flancare Park	7.30pm

SERIES Nº 33

Friday 18th November	Waterford United vs Drogheda United at R.S.C.	7.30pm
Friday 18th November	Bohemians vs Shelbourne at Dalymount Park	7.45pm
Friday 18th November	Cork City vs Derry City at Turner's Cross	7.45pm
Friday 18th November	St. Patrick's Athletic vs Longford Town at Richmond Park	7.45pm
Friday 18th November	U.C. Dublin vs Shamrock Rovers at Belfield Park	7.45pm
Saturday 19th November	Finn Harps vs Bray Wanderers at Finn Park	7.45pm

THE FOOTBALL ASSOCIATION OF IRELAND (FAI)

Founded
1921

Address 80 Merrion Square, Dublin 2

Phone (01) 703-7500

Fax (01) 661-0931

Website www.fai.ie

Eircom FAI First Division Clubs for 2005

ATHLONE TOWN FC

Founded: 1887
Former Names: None
Nickname: 'Town'
Ground: St. Mel's Park, Glenavon Road, Athlone, Co Westmeath
Record Attendance: 9,000 (vs AC Milan)
Pitch Size: 110 × 71 yards

Colours: Blue & Black striped shirts with Black shorts
Telephone Nº: (090) 649-8649
Fax Number: (090) 649-8838
Ground Capacity: 3,000
Seating Capacity: 200
Web Site: www.athlonetownfc.com

GENERAL INFORMATION

Car Parking: Small car park at the ground
Coach Parking: In the Town Centre
Nearest Railway Station: Athlone (¼ mile)
Nearest Bus Station: Athlone (¼ mile)
Club Shop: At the ground
Opening Times: Matchdays only
Telephone Nº: (090) 649-8649

ADMISSION INFO (2005 PRICES)

Adult Standing: € 10.00
Adult Seating: € 10.00
Senior Citizen/Junior Standing: € 3.00
Senior Citizen/Junior Seating: € 3.00
Programme Price: € 2.00

DISABLED INFORMATION

Wheelchairs: Accommodated
Helpers: Admitted
Prices: € 10.00 each for both the disabled and helpers
Disabled Toilets: None
Contact: (090) 649-8649 (Bookings are necessary)

Travelling Supporters' Information:
Routes: Take the N55/N6/N61 to Athlone. The ground is situated just off the N55 to the north of the town. Exit the M55 at Junction 4 and turn left then turn off at the mini-roundabout into Grace Park Road and pass under the railway bridge. Bear right at the end of the road and the ground is on the right.

COBH RAMBLERS FC

Founded: 1922
Former Names: Cove Ramblers FC
Nickname: 'Ramblers' 'Rams'
Ground: St. Colman's Park, Glenanaar Place, Cobh, Co. Cork
Record Attendance: 6,612 (vs Finn Harps)
Pitch Size: 108 × 78 yards

Colours: Claret and Blue shirts with White shorts
Telephone Nº: (021) 481-2371
Office Nº: (021) 481-3078
Ground Capacity: 9,000
Seating Capacity: 362
Web Site: www.cobhramblers.com
Correspondence Address: c/o 17 Elmwood Grove, Cobh, Co. Cork

GENERAL INFORMATION
Car Parking: Street parking only
Coach Parking: At the ground
Nearest Railway Station: Cobh (1 mile)
Nearest Bus Station: Cork
Club Shop: At the ground
Opening Times: Matchdays only
Telephone Nº: (021) 481-3078

ADMISSION INFO (2005 PRICES)
Adult Standing: € 10.00
Adult Seating: € 10.00
Senior Citizen/Junior Standing: € 5.00
Senior Citizen/Junior Seating: € 5.00
Under-16s: Admitted free with ID Card – Otherwise € 2.00
Programme Price: € 2.00

DISABLED INFORMATION
Wheelchairs: Accommodated
Helpers: Admitted
Prices: Free of charge for the disabled and their helpers
Disabled Toilets: None
Contact: (021) 481-3078 (Bookings are necessary)

Travelling Supporters' Information:
Routes: Approaching from Cork City or Waterford: Branch off before Carrigtwohill village on the dual carriageway roundabout to Cobh and keep on the right to the Belvelly Bridge just beyond the Fota Wildlife Park entrance. Turn right and keep to the right for 4½ miles, in the process passing the IFI Fertiliser Plant and Verolme Dockyard. Take the second turning on the left after the Filling Station on the Lake Road and follow the direct route for ½ mile on rising ground. On reaching level ground take the fourth exit on the left hand side, St. Colman's Park is visible by the floodlight pylons.

DUBLIN CITY FC

Founded: 1928
Former Names: Home Farm Drumcondra FC,
Home Farm Everton FC and Home Farm FC
Nickname: 'Vikings'
Ground: Tolka Park, Richmond Road, Drumcondra,
Dublin 3
Record Attendance: 9,000 (vs Bohemians)

Pitch Size: 110 × 75 yards
Colours: Navy Blue shirts and shorts
Telephone Nº: (01) 837-7777
Fax Number: (01) 836-7821
Ground Capacity: 9,680
Seating Capacity: 9,680
Web Site: www.dublincityfc.net

GENERAL INFORMATION

Car Parking: Street parking only
Coach Parking: Street parking only
Nearest Railway Station: Amiens Street
Nearest Bus Stop: Richmond Road, Drumcondra
Club Shop: None, but merchandise is available via all
Carrolls Irish Gift Stores
Office address: 120 Upper Drumcondra Road, Dublin 9

ADMISSION INFO (2005 PRICES)

Adult Seating: € 10.00
Senior Citizen/Junior Seating: € 5.00
Specials: Reduced family rates are available on request
Programme Price: € 2.00

DISABLED INFORMATION

Wheelchairs: Accommodated
Helpers: Admitted
Prices: € 5.00 each for both the disabled and helpers
Disabled Toilets: Available
Contact: (01) 837-7777   (Bookings are necessary)

Travelling Supporters' Information:
Routes: From the City Centre: Take the N1 (Belfast) road to Drumcondra and the ground is situated in Richmond Road, adjacent
to Holy Cross College over the Drumcondra bridge.

DUNDALK FC

Founded: 1903
Former Names: GNR FC and Dundalk Rovers FC
Nickname: 'Lilywhites'
Ground: Oriel Park, Carrick Road, Dundalk, Co. Louth
Record Attendance: 22,000
Pitch Size: 108 × 85 yards

Colours: Black and White striped shirts, Black shorts
Telephone Nº: (042) 933-5894
Fax Number: (042) 933-0003
Ground Capacity: 11,000
Seating Capacity: 1,500
Web Site: www.dundalkfc.com

GENERAL INFORMATION

Car Parking: Street parking only
Coach Parking: At the ground
Nearest Railway Station: Dundalk (adjacent)
Nearest Bus Station: Dundalk (½ mile)
Club Shop: At the ground
Opening Times: Matchdays only
Telephone Nº: (042) 933-5894

ADMISSION INFO (2005 PRICES)

Adult Standing: € 8.00
Adult Seating: € 12.00
Senior Citizen/Junior Standing: € 5.00
Senior Citizen/Junior Seating: € 6.00
Under-12s: € 2.00 – € 3.00
Programme Price: € 2.00

DISABLED INFORMATION

Wheelchairs: Accommodated
Helpers: Admitted
Prices: Normal prices apply for the disabled and helpers
Disabled Toilets: Available
Contact: (042) 933-5894 (Bookings are not necessary)

Travelling Supporters' Information:
Routes: From the North: Pass through the Town Centre and turn right at the fourth set of traffic lights. Take the second exit at the roundabout past the 'Harp Brewery' (which is on the right) and Oriel Park is situated on the left hand side after approximately 200 metres; From Dublin: Enter Dundalk and turn left at the 3rd set of traffic lights. Take the 2nd exit at the roundabout then follow directions as From the North above; From Ardee: Enter Dundalk then turn left at the Crescent Garda Barracks past the Harp Brewery. Oriel Park is on the left hand side after approximately 200 metres.

GALWAY UNITED FC

Founded: 1937
Former Names: Galway Rovers FC
Nickname: 'The Tribesmen'
Ground: Terryland Park, Dyke Road, Galway
Record Attendance: 7,260 (vs Cork City)
Pitch Size: 110 × 75 yards

Colours: Maroon shirts and shorts
Telephone Nº: (091) 779555
Fax Number: (091) 777045
Ground Capacity: 5,000
Seating Capacity: 1,400
Web Site: www.galwayunitedfc.ie

GENERAL INFORMATION

Car Parking: 200 spaces available at the ground
Coach Parking: At the ground
Nearest Railway Station: Ceannt (1½ miles)
Nearest Bus Station: Eyre Square (1½ miles)
Club Shop: At the ground
Opening Times: Matchdays only
Telephone Nº: (091) 779555

ADMISSION INFO (2005 PRICES)

Adult Standing: € 10.00
Adult Seating: € 10.00
Senior Citizen/Junior Standing: € 6.00
Senior Citizen/Junior Seating: € 6.00
Under-16s: € 4.00
Programme Price: € 2.00

DISABLED INFORMATION

Wheelchairs: Accommodated
Helpers: Admitted
Prices: Normal prices apply for the disabled and helpers
Disabled Toilets: Available
Contact: (091) 779555 (Bookings are necessary)

Travelling Supporters' Information:
Routes: Follow the N6 dual carriageway to the roundabout at Terryland Shopping Centre (Dunnes Stores). Take the 2nd exit into Headford Road, first right after the McDonalds Drive Thru' and Omniplex cinema. Pass the Blackbox Theatre. The ground is at the top of this road – after travelling under the flyover, Terryland Park is on the right. To avoid going under the low flyover, buses should take the 3rd exit off the roundabout adjacent to the Holiday Inn. Then go to the T-junction and turn left onto Dyke Road. Terryland Park is then at the bottom of the hill on the left.

KILDARE COUNTY FC

Kildare County FC are currently playing at the Newbridge Town FC ground in Station Road.

Founded: 2002
Former Names: None
Nickname: 'The Thoroughbreds'
Ground: Station Road, Newbridge, Co. Kildare
Record Attendance: Approximately 2,500
Pitch Size: 110 × 72 yards

Colours: White shirts with Black shorts
Telephone Nº: (045) 487724
Fax Number: (045) 449546
Ground Capacity: 2,500
Seating Capacity: 250
Web Site: www.kildarecountyfc.com

GENERAL INFORMATION
Car Parking: At the ground
Coach Parking: At the ground
Nearest Railway Station: Newbridge (¼ mile)
Nearest Bus Station: Newbridge
Club Shop: At the ground
Opening Times: Matchdays only
Telephone Nº: (045) 487724

ADMISSION INFO (2005 PRICES)
Adult Standing: € 10.00
Adult Seating: € 10.00
Senior Citizen Standing/Seating: Free of charge
Junior Standing: € 5.00
Junior Seating: € 5.00
Under-14s: € 3.00 when accompanied by an adult
Programme Price: € 2.00

DISABLED INFORMATION
Wheelchairs: Accommodated
Helpers: Admitted
Prices: Free of charge for both the disabled and helpers
Disabled Toilets: Available
Contact: (045) 487724   (Bookings are necessary)

Travelling Supporters' Information:
Routes: From Dublin: Take the N7 motorway past Naas and take the exit for Newbridge. Upon entering Newbridge, cross the Liffey bridge and travel up Main Street then turn right at the post office into Charlotte Street for Station Road. Cross the bridge at the train station and the football ground is on the left; From the South: Take the motorway then leave that the exit for the Curragh, heading into Newbridge. Travel up through the town and turn left at the post office into Station Road. Then as above.

KILKENNY CITY FC

Founded: 1966
Former Names: EMFA FC
Nickname: 'The Cats'
Ground: Buckley Park, Callan Road, Kilkenny
Record Attendance: 6,500
Pitch Size: 107 × 78 yards

Colours: Yellow shirts with Black shorts
Telephone Nº: (056) 775-1888
Fax Number: (056) 772-1414
Ground Capacity: 5,000
Seating Capacity: 1,500
Web Site: www.kilkennycityfc.com

GENERAL INFORMATION
Car Parking: At the ground
Coach Parking: At the ground
Nearest Railway Station: Kilkenny (2½ miles)
Nearest Bus Station: Kilkenny (2½ miles)
Club Shop: At the ground
Opening Times: Matchdays only
Telephone Nº: (056) 775-1888

ADMISSION INFO (2005 PRICES)
Adult Standing: € 10.00
Adult Seating: € 10.00
Senior Citizen/Junior Standing: € 5.00
Senior Citizen/Junior Seating: € 5.00
Under-12s: Free of charge
Programme Price: € 3.00

DISABLED INFORMATION
Wheelchairs: Accommodated
Helpers: Admitted
Prices: Free of charge for both the disabled and helpers
Disabled Toilets: Available
Contact: (086) 339-8310   (Bookings are necessary)

Travelling Supporters' Information:
Routes: Buckley Park is situated on the N76 Callan/Clonmel Road, 1½ miles outside of the City. Approaching from Kilkenny it is on the right hand side of the road down a small lane.

LIMERICK FC

Founded: 1937
Former Names: Limerick City FC
Nickname: 'Blues'
Ground: Hogan Park, Rathbane, Limerick
Record Attendance: 5,500
Pitch Size: 115 × 76 yards

Colours: Blue shirts and shorts
Telephone Nº: (061) 340264
Fax Number: (061) 340264
Ground Capacity: 3,000
Seating Capacity: 610
Web Site: None

GENERAL INFORMATION
Car Parking: At the ground
Coach Parking: At the ground
Nearest Railway Station: Colbert (1½ miles)
Nearest Bus Station: Colbert
Club Shop: At the ground
Opening Times: Matchdays only
Telephone Nº: (061) 340264

ADMISSION INFO (2005 PRICES)
Adult Standing: € 12.00
Adult Seating: € 12.00
Senior Citizen/Junior Standing: € 6.00
Senior Citizen/Junior Seating: € 6.00
Programme Price: € 3.00

DISABLED INFORMATION
Wheelchairs: Accommodated
Helpers: Admitted
Prices: Normal prices apply for the disabled and helpers
Disabled Toilets: Available
Contact: (061) 340264 (Bookings are necessary)

Travelling Supporters' Information:
Routes: Take the N7 from Dublin into Limerick then turn left at the roundabout by the Parkway Shopping Centre. Continue straight ahead at the next three roundabouts then take the 2nd left at 'Pulse' hairdressers and the ground is straight ahead.

MONAGHAN UNITED FC

Founded: 1979
Former Names: None
Nickname: 'The Mons'
Ground: Century Homes Park, Newbliss Road, Monaghan
Record Attendance: 2,000
Pitch Size: 110 × 74 yards

Colours: White shirts with Blue shorts
Telephone Nº: (047) 84798
Fax Number: (047) 72599
Ground Capacity: 5,000
Seating Capacity: 620
Web Site: www.monaghanunited.ie

GENERAL INFORMATION
Car Parking: At the ground
Coach Parking: At the ground
Nearest Railway Station: Dundalk (32 miles)
Nearest Bus Station: Monaghan (1 mile)
Club Shop: At the ground
Opening Times: Matchdays only
Telephone Nº: (047) 84798

ADMISSION INFO (2005 PRICES)
Adult Standing: € 10.00
Adult Seating: € 10.00
Senior Citizen/Junior Standing: € 5.00
Senior Citizen/Junior Seating: € 5.00
Under-11s: Admitted free of charge with a paying adult
Programme Price: € 2.00

DISABLED INFORMATION
Wheelchairs: Accommodated
Helpers: Admitted
Prices: Normal prices apply for the disabled and helpers
Disabled Toilets: Available
Contact: (047) 84798   (Bookings are not necessary)

Travelling Supporters' Information:
Routes: The ground is situated 1 mile from Monaghan town on the N54 to Clones. Turn left for Threemilehouse/Newbliss and the ground is 100 yards along on the left hand side.

SLIGO ROVERS FC

Founded: 1928
Former Names: None
Nickname: 'Rovers' or 'Bit of Red'
Ground: The Showgrounds, Sligo
Record Attendance: 9,000 (vs Shamrock Rovers)
Pitch Size: 110 × 75 yards

Colours: Red shirts and shorts
Telephone N°: (071) 917-1212
Fax Number: (071) 917-1331
Ground Capacity: 6,000
Seating Capacity: 700
Web Site: www.sligorovers.com

GENERAL INFORMATION
Car Parking: None near to the ground
Coach Parking: Cathedral Street
Nearest Railway Station: Sligo
Nearest Bus Station: Sligo
Club Shop: At the ground
Opening Times: Matchdays only
Telephone N°: (071) 71212

Correspondence Address: P.O. Box 275, Sligo

ADMISSION INFO (2005 PRICES)
Adult Standing: € 10.00
Adult Seating: € 10.00
Senior Citizen/Junior Standing: € 5.00
Senior Citizen/Junior Seating: € 5.00
Under-12s: € 3.00
Programme Price: € 2.50

DISABLED INFORMATION
Wheelchairs: Accommodated in the disabled section
Helpers: Admitted
Prices: Normal prices apply for the disabled and helpers
Disabled Toilets: Available
Contact: (071) 917-1212 (Bookings are necessary)

Travelling Supporters' Information:
Routes: From Derry/Donegal: Enter the town on the Ballyshannon Road, cross over the river and process to the traffic lights at the Adelaide Street/Wine Street junction. Proceed into Adelaide Street and park at the Adelaide Street car park (with Dunnes Stores on the left); From Leitrim/Fermanagh: Upon entering Sligo, follow the one way traffic system until you reach the Wine Street car park about half way down the street; From the East, West or South: All roads converge at Ballisodare (5 miles from Sligo). From there, drive into town and proceed down Pearse Road until reaching a sign which says 'Heavy Good Vehicles' this way (an arrow points the direction). Travel down Mail Coach Road until reaching the traffic lights. Continue straight on until reaching the Cathedral (on the right). Parking is available here or go straight on to Adelaide Street for parking.
Route from the Wine Street/Adelaide Street Car Parks: Walk up towards the Cathedral and turn right into John Street at the traffic lights. Continue straight on for the ground; Route from the Cathedral: Turn left into John Street at the traffic lights for the ground; Route from the Railway/Bus Station: Cross the road into Wolfe Tone Street. Walk to the end then turn right and continue straight on for the ground.

FIRST DIVISION STATISTICS

Home & Away Score Charts

and

Final League Tables

1995-96

	Division One	Pd	Wn	Dw	Ls	GF	GA	Pts	
1.	Bray Wanderers AFC (Bray)	27	16	7	4	53	21	55	P
2.	Finn Harps FC (Ballybofey)	27	14	7	6	50	25	49	P
3.	Home Farm-Everton FC (Dublin)	27	14	4	9	44	33	46	PO
4.	Cobh Ramblers FC (Cobh)	27	10	13	4	30	18	43	
5.	St. James's Gate AFC (Dublin)	27	9	11	7	35	30	38	
6.	Limerick FC (Limerick)	27	10	6	11	38	34	36	
7.	Kilkenny City FC (Kilkenny)	27	9	8	10	32	35	35	
8.	Waterford United FC (Waterford)	27	9	7	11	37	39	34	
9.	Longford Town FC (Longford)	27	5	6	16	25	49	21	
10	Monaghan United FC (Monaghan)	27	2	5	20	11	71	11	
		270	98	74	98	355	355	368	

Home Farm FC (Dublin) changed to Home Farm-Everton FC (Dublin) under a player-exchange deal with English club Everton FC (Liverpool).

1996-97

Promotion/Relegation Play-off

Dundalk FC (Dundalk)	3-0, 0-1	Waterford United FC (Waterford)

	Division One	Pd	Wn	Dw	Ls	GF	GA	Pts	
1.	Kilkenny City FC (Kilkenny)	27	15	10	2	47	20	55	P
2.	Drogheda United FC (Drogheda)	27	12	8	7	44	27	44	P
3.	Waterford United FC (Waterford)	27	12	8	7	41	28	44	PO
4.	Athlone Town AFC (Athlone)	27	10	7	10	40	39	37	
5.	Cobh Ramblers FC (Cobh)	27	9	8	10	34	28	35	
6.	Galway United FC (Galway)	27	9	8	10	33	38	35	
7.	Longford Town FC (Longford)	27	7	13	7	31	38	34	
8.	Monaghan United FC(Monaghan)	27	7	9	11	30	46	30	
9.	St. Francis FC (Dublin)	27	7	7	13	20	33	28	*
10	Limerick FC (Limerick)	27	4	8	13	23	55	20	
		270	92	86	92	352	352	362	

*   St. James's Gate AFC (Dublin) were expelled from the league pre-season as they were unable to meet financial guarantees. Their place was awarded to St. Francis FC (Dublin).

1997-98

League of Ireland Division One 1997-98	Athlone Town	Bray Wanderers	Cobh Ramblers	Galway United	Home Farm-Ev.	Limerick AFC	Longford Town	Monaghan Utd.	St. Francis FC	Waterford Utd/
Athlone Town AFC (Athlone)	■		2-4	2-0					1-1	0-1
	■	1-2	2-0	2-1	0-1	1-1	2-0	2-1	1-4	0-1
Bray Wanderers AFC (Bray)	1-1	■	0-0		0-1			1-0	2-1	
	2-1	■	7-0	2-1	2-0	3-2	4-0	4-0	1-0	0-1
Cobh Ramblers FC (Cobh)			■	1-1			2-0	2-1	1-3	0-1
	2-1	0-1	■	1-0	1-0	2-1	1-0	0-1	2-3	1-2
Galway United FC (Galway)		1-0		■		2-1		2-0	1-0	
	2-1	1-4	4-1	■	2-1	2-2	1-0	3-1	5-0	0-1
Home Farm-Everton FC (Dublin)	4-1		0-1	0-0	■	0-0	0-0			
	1-2	0-0	2-1	1-1	■	1-2	1-0	2-1	1-1	3-0
Limerick AFC (Limerick)	1-1	2-1	2-2			■	6-0			
	0-0	1-0	1-0	1-0	1-1	■	1-0	3-1	2-0	1-2
Longford Town FC (Longford)	1-2	1-3		0-2			■	0-4		0-2
	2-2	1-0	2-2	1-2	0-1	0-2	■	0-2	1-1	0-0
Monaghan United FC (Monaghan)	1-1				0-0	1-2		■		0-2
	0-2	0-2	2-1	2-1	3-3	1-2	1-3	■	1-2	1-2
St. Francis FC (Dublin)					0-2	0-2	2-0	0-0	■	
	1-0	4-3	1-3	1-2	1-1	1-2	0-0	0-1	■	1-4
Waterford United FC (Waterford)		1-3		2-1	1-1	0-0			0-0	■
	2-0	0-3	1-1	1-0	1-0	3-0	1-0	2-0	1-1	■

Promotion/Relegation Play-off   (05/05/98 – 08/05/98)

University College Dublin AFC (Dublin)　　　　2-1, 3-1　　　　　　　　Limerick FC (Limerick)

	Division One	**Pd**	**Wn**	**Dw**	**Ls**	**GF**	**GA**	**Pts**	
1.	Waterford United FC (Waterford)	27	18	6	3	35	17	60	P
2.	Bray Wanderers AFC (Bray)	27	17	3	7	51	21	54	P
3.	Limerick FC (Limerick)	27	14	8	5	41	25	50	PO
4.	Galway United FC (Galway)	27	13	4	10	38	29	43	
5.	Home Farm-Everton FC (Dublin)	27	9	11	7	28	22	38	
6.	Cobh Ramblers FC (Cobh)	27	10	5	12	32	41	35	
7.	Athlone Town AFC (Athlone)	27	8	7	12	31	37	31	
8.	St. Francis FC (Dublin)	27	7	8	12	29	40	29	
9.	Monaghan United FC (Monaghan)	27	6	4	17	26	44	22	
10	Longford Town FC (Longford)	27	2	6	19	12	47	12	
		270	104	62	104	323	323	374	

1998-99

League of Ireland Division One 1998-99	Athlone Town AFC	Cobh Ramblers FC	Drogheda United FC	Galway United FC	Home Farm-Everton FC	Kilkenny City FC	Limerick AFC	Longford Town FC	Monaghan United FC	St. Francis FC
Athlone Town AFC (Athlone)		2-3	0-1	1-1	1-1	2-0	1-1	1-1	4-1	1-1
		1-0	1-2	2-2	3-1	2-2	0-2	3-1	3-0	2-0
Cobh Ramblers FC (Cobh)	2-2		1-2	0-3	2-2	4-0	1-1	2-0	1-1	2-0
	4-0		2-0	3-0	2-1	3-1	1-0	0-2	3-0	4-1
Drogheda United FC (Drogheda)	1-1	4-1		0-2	3-2	1-0	1-1	1-0	1-1	2-2
	4-0	1-1		1-1	1-0	0-1	1-0	1-2	2-0	1-1
Galway United FC (Galway)	4-0	2-0	2-1		2-1	0-0	2-1	0-0	3-0	2-0
	2-0	0-2	2-2		2-1	1-0	0-0	0-0	1-1	1-1
Home Farm-Everton FC (Dublin)	2-1	0-1	0-2	2-3		1-2	1-2	1-3	1-1	2-0
	3-0	2-3	1-5	0-2		2-1	3-1	2-0	2-1	3-2
Kilkenny City FC (Kilkenny)	4-1	3-1	1-1	1-1	1-0		2-1	2-2	0-2	1-0
	1-2	0-2	2-2	4-2	1-0		1-1	3-1	3-3	2-2
Limerick AFC (Limerick)	3-1	1-1	1-0	1-1	0-1	1-1		0-0	1-1	2-1
	3-2	3-0	0-3	0-1	1-0	0-2		2-0	1-0	3-0
Longford Town FC (Longford)	0-1	0-1	1-1	1-1	1-0	1-0	0-1		2-1	2-0
	1-0	2-0	1-2	1-1	2-0	3-1	3-0		2-0	2-3
Monaghan United FC (Monaghan)	1-0	2-0	1-1	2-0	0-0	1-1	0-1	2-1		4-0
	5-1	1-0	0-0	3-3	1-1	0-1	1-1	0-1		3-1
St. Francis FC (Dublin)	0-2	2-2	0-3	0-1	0-1	0-1	0-0	0-0	1-1	
	1-1	1-0	0-3	2-2	1-2	0-3	2-2	0-2	0-3	

Promotion/Relegation Play-off   (05/05/99 – 08/05/99)

Cobh Ramblers FC (Cobh)   0-5, 0-2   Bohemian FC (Dublin)

	Division One	**Pd**	**Wn**	**Dw**	**Ls**	**GF**	**GA**	**Pts**	
1.	Drogheda United FC (Drogheda)	36	17	13	6	57	32	64	P
2.	Galway United FC (Galway)	36	16	16	4	53	34	64	P
3.	Cobh Ramblers FC (Cobh)	36	17	7	12	55	43	58	PO
4.	Longford Town FC (Longford)	36	15	9	12	41	33	54	
5.	Kilkenny City FC (Kilkenny)	36	14	11	11	49	46	53	
6.	Limerick FC (Limerick)	36	13	13	10	39	35	52	
7.	Monaghan United FC (Monaghan)	36	10	14	12	44	44	44	
8.	Athlone Town AFC (Athlone)	36	10	10	16	45	61	40	
9.	Home Farm-Everton FC (Dublin)	36	11	5	20	42	54	38	*
10.	St. Francis FC (Dublin)	36	2	12	22	25	68	18	
		360	125	110	125	450	450	485	

*   Home Farm-Everton FC (Dublin) severed their link with English club Everton FC (Liverpool) and changed their name to Home Farm-Fingal FC (Dublin) for next season.

1999-2000

League of Ireland Division One 1999-2000	Athlone Town	Bray Wanderers	Cobh Ramblers	Dundalk FC	Home Farm-Fingal	Kilkenny City FC	Limerick AFC	Longford Town	Monaghan United	St. Francis FC
Athlone Town AFC (Athlone)		1-1	1-0	0-0	1-0	0-1	3-0	1-1	2-0	0-0
		0-2	2-2	1-1	0-0	1-1	1-2	1-1	2-2	1-0
Bray Wanderers AFC (Bray)	3-1		2-2	0-1	5-1	1-0	2-1	1-1	5-2	2-0
	2-1		5-0	2-3	3-0	2-1	3-2	1-0	1-0	1-0
Cobh Ramblers FC (Cobh)	1-0	0-3		0-3	1-0	3-1	2-1	0-2	6-4	2-0
	1-0	2-0		0-1	0-1	2-3	2-1	1-6	1-0	2-2
Dundalk FC (Dundalk)	0-1	1-1	1-1		2-0	1-0	2-1	4-1	0-2	0-0
	1-0	1-2	2-1		2-0	2-1	2-0	0-1	0-1	1-2
Home Farm-Fingal FC (Dublin)	1-0	2-2	2-0	1-2		2-2	1-2	3-2	3-0	2-1
	1-0	0-3	2-2	0-1		0-1	2-2	1-2	2-2	0-1
Kilkenny City FC (Kilkenny)	4-1	1-0	0-1	2-0	2-2		1-0	2-1	2-2	1-0
	5-1	5-1	0-1	1-2	1-0		3-2	2-1	2-1	5-0
Limerick AFC (Limerick)	1-1	1-2	1-0	1-3	3-1	0-0		0-3	2-0	0-1
	1-1	0-0	3-3	2-1	1-1	0-3		0-2	2-2	1-1
Longford Town FC (Longford)	3-1	2-4	2-1	1-1	4-1	3-1	2-0		4-1	1-2
	1-0	2-2	2-1	1-0	2-2	1-1	2-1		3-1	2-1
Monaghan United FC (Monaghan)	0-1	3-1	1-2	3-2	2-2	1-3	5-2	0-1		0-0
	2-2	0-0	1-4	1-2	2-1	1-5	0-0	0-4		1-1
St. Francis FC (Dublin)	1-1	0-3	1-2	0-2	2-2	0-4	0-0	0-3	1-1	
	0-1	1-1	1-1	0-3	2-4	0-0	2-1	2-1	2-2	

Promotion/Relegation Play-off   (03/05/00 + 06/05/00)

Kilkenny City FC (Kilkenny)   1-0, 1-0   Waterford United FC (Waterford)

	Division One	**Pd**	**Wn**	**Dw**	**Ls**	**GF**	**GA**	**Pts**	
1.	Bray Wanderers AFC (Bray)	36	21	9	6	69	38	72	P
2.	Longford Town FC (Longford)	36	21	7	8	71	40	70	P
3.	Kilkenny City FC (Kilkenny)	36	20	7	9	65	34	67	PO
4.	Dundalk FC (Dundalk)	36	20	6	10	50	31	66	
5.	Cobh Ramblers FC (Cobh)	36	14	8	14	52	59	50	
6.	Athlone Town AFC (Athlone)	36	8	14	14	31	42	38	
7.	Home Farm-Fingal FC (Dublin)	36	8	11	17	43	60	35	
8.	Fingal-St. Francis FC (Dublin)	36	6	14	15	28	54	33	*
9.	Monaghan United FC (Monaghan)	36	6	12	18	46	73	30	
10	Limerick FC (Limerick)	36	6	11	19	36	60	29	
		360	130	100	130	489	489	490	

Cobh Ramblers FC 0-0 Kilkenny City on 23/10/99 was abandoned after 40 minutes due to floodlight failure. The match was replayed on 01/12/99 finishing Cobh Ramblers FC 2-3 Kilkenny City.

Kilkenny City 3-2 Limerick on 12/11/99 result was annulled as Kilkenny fielded an ineligible player. The match was replayed on 20/04/00 ending 1-0 but this match was disputed and a civil judge ruled that it should never have been played. As a result, the scoreline of the original match was reinstated.

* St. Francis FC (Dublin) changed their name to Fingal-St. Francis FC (Dublin)

2000-2001

League of Ireland Division One 2000-2001	Athlone Town	Cobh Ramblers	Drogheda United	Dundalk FC	Home Farm-Fingal	Limerick AFC	Monaghan United	St. Francis FC	Sligo Rovers FC	Waterford AFC
Athlone Town AFC (Athlone)		1-0	0-0	1-2	1-2	1-0	2-3	2-0	1-1	0-0
		2-0	2-1	1-1	5-2	2-2	2-1	3-0	0-0	1-0
Cobh Ramblers FC (Cobh)	2-0		2-2	2-0	6-1	1-3	2-2	1-0	0-2	1-1
	1-5		2-1	3-2	0-1	3-1	0-1	1-0	1-4	0-2
Drogheda United FC (Drogheda)	1-2	2-0		0-3	0-2	1-1	1-1	1-0	0-1	0-2
	1-4	3-1		0-3	1-1	2-1	2-4	1-1	1-3	0-2
Dundalk FC (Dundalk)	2-1	3-2	1-0		0-1	0-0	1-0	7-0	2-5	1-0
	3-0	2-2	1-0		3-1	1-1	2-0	2-0	3-1	1-0
Home Farm-Fingal FC (Dublin)	0-0	1-0	0-0	1-2		1-1	0-0	1-0	4-1	1-1
	1-2	2-2	3-2	2-1		1-5	2-4	2-2	3-2	3-3
Limerick AFC (Limerick)	0-1	1-0	1-0	0-2	1-0		0-2	1-0	2-0	1-1
	0-0	0-2	3-1	1-1	0-0		2-0	1-4	2-1	1-1
Monaghan United FC (Monaghan)	3-1	0-0	2-0	4-0	1-0	2-0		1-1	1-1	0-0
	1-2	2-1	1-0	1-1	2-2	3-1		3-1	0-3	1-2
St. Francis FC (Dublin)	0-1	3-0	1-1	1-1	1-1	2-1	3-5		0-3	0-2
	1-1	0-1	1-1	2-6	0-0	0-2	1-2		1-2	1-1
Sligo Rovers FC (Sligo)	4-2	3-2	2-0	1-1	1-0	1-0	1-2	1-0		1-3
	1-2	1-0	1-0	2-1	3-0	2-2	1-2	2-1		1-4
Waterford United FC (Waterford)	0-0	3-1	4-0	1-2	3-0	0-1	0-0	1-1	2-0	
	1-2	3-1	3-1	1-1	2-0	0-1	2-2	2-0	3-2	

Promotion/Relegation Play-off

Athlone Town AFC (Athlone)   2-1, 1-2 (aet)   (4-2 on penalties)   University College Dublin AFC

	Division One	Pd	Wn	Dw	Ls	GF	GA	Pts	
1.	Dundalk FC (Dundalk)	36	20	9	7	65	38	69	P
2.	Monaghan United FC (Monaghan)	36	18	11	7	59	40	65	P
3.	Athlone Town AFC (Athlone)	36	18	10	8	53	37	64	PO
4.	Sligo Rovers FC (Sligo)	36	19	5	12	61	48	62	
5.	Waterford United FC (Waterford)	36	16	13	7	56	30	61	
6.	Limerick FC (Limerick)	36	13	11	12	40	39	50	
7.	Home Farm-Fingal FC (Dublin)	36	10	13	13	43	58	43	*
8.	Cobh Ramblers FC (Cobh)	36	10	6	20	43	60	36	
9.	Drogheda United FC (Drogheda)	36	4	9	23	27	62	21	
10.	Fingal-St. Francis FC (Dublin)	36	3	11	22	29	64	20	
		360	131	98	131	476	476	491	

*   Home Farm-Fingal FC (Dublin) changed their club name to Dublin City FC (Dublin) for next season.

League of Ireland Division One 2001-2002	Athlone Town	Cobh Ramblers	Drogheda United	Dublin City FC	Finn Harps FC	Kilkenny City FC	Limerick AFC	Sligo Rovers FC	Waterford AFC
Athlone Town AFC (Athlone)		2-1	2-2	1-2	0-2	1-4	0-2	2-0	1-1
		1-1	0-0	0-2	2-1	0-0	4-1	3-3	0-1
Cobh Ramblers FC (Cobh)	4-2		0-0	1-2	1-2	0-1	0-2	1-1	0-0
	0-4		0-1	1-0	0-1	0-1	1-2	3-0	0-2
Drogheda United FC (Drogheda)	2-0	3-1		6-1	2-0	0-0	4-2	2-1	0-0
	2-2	1-0		1-3	1-1	1-0	2-0	5-0	2-2
Dublin City FC (Dublin)	2-1	1-2	2-2		3-1	2-1	4-0	1-2	1-2
	1-1	0-2	1-1		3-3	4-4	1-0	2-2	3-1
Finn Harps FC (Ballybofey)	3-1	3-1	1-1	0-1		3-3	1-0	1-1	2-0
	2-1	0-0	3-3	1-0		2-2	5-3	0-3	1-2
Kilkenny City FC (Kilkenny)	4-1	2-1	1-2	0-2	3-0		1-0	3-1	0-3
	4-1	1-2	1-0	3-2	2-3		4-1	0-2	0-0
Limerick AFC (Limerick)	1-2	0-1	0-0	1-1	0-1	1-0		2-1	3-4
	2-2	1-1	0-3	3-2	0-0	1-0		0-5	4-0
Sligo Rovers FC (Sligo)	1-1	2-1	0-1	0-1	0-1	1-0	0-0		1-2
	1-0	0-3	1-1	2-3	0-2	1-1	0-0		3-1
Waterford United FC (Waterford)	1-2	1-0	2-2	1-1	5-0	1-1	2-0	3-0	
	0-0	3-3	0-0	0-1	3-4	0-0	2-0	2-0	

Promotion/Relegation Play-off

Longford Town FC (Longford)	1-0, 2-3 (aet)	Finn Harps FC (Ballybofey)

(Longford Town FC won 6-5 on penalties)

	Division One	**Pd**	**Wn**	**Dw**	**Ls**	**GF**	**GA**	**Pts**	
1.	Drogheda United FC (Drogheda)	32	14	16	2	53	28	58	P
2.	Finn Harps FC (Ballybofey)	32	15	9	8	51	47	54	PO
3.	Dublin City FC (Dublin)	32	15	8	9	55	46	53	
4.	Waterford United FC (Waterford)	32	13	12	7	47	35	48	*
5.	Kilkenny City FC (Kilkenny)	32	12	9	11	47	39	45	
6.	Sligo Rovers FC (Sligo)	32	8	9	15	35	48	33	
7.	Athlone Town AFC (Athlone)	32	7	11	14	40	53	32	
8.	Cobh Ramblers FC (Cobh)	32	8	7	17	32	42	31	
9.	Limerick FC (Limerick)	32	8	7	17	32	54	31	
		288	100	88	100	392	392	355	

* Waterford United FC (Waterford) had 3 points deducted for fielding an ineligible player.

Fingal-St. Francis FC (Dublin) were taken over by and merged into St. Patrick's Athletic FC (Dublin) prior to the start of the season. This occurred too late to find a replacement club for the season.

Elected: Kildare County FC (Newbridge)

Premier Division reduced to 10 clubs and Division One extended to 12 clubs for next season

2002-2003

League of Ireland Division One 2002-2003	Athlone Town	Cobh Ramblers	Dublin City FC	Dundalk FC	Finn Harps FC	Galway United	Kildare County	Kilkenny City	Limerick AFC	Monaghan Utd.	Sligo Rovers	Waterford AFC
Athlone Town AFC		1-3	2-1	2-0	0-0	0-3	1-2	1-1	1-3	0-0	2-2	2-3
Cobh Ramblers FC	3-1		1-3	0-0	1-1	2-0	1-1	3-2	3-2	3-2	2-1	2-3
Dublin City FC	2-1	3-2		2-4	0-2	2-0	2-0	3-4	0-1	3-2	1-2	5-1
Dundalk FC	2-4	2-2	2-2		3-1	0-4	0-2	0-0	1-1	1-2	1-3	0-1
Finn Harps FC	4-0	1-2	2-0	2-1		1-3	1-2	2-0	3-0	3-1	3-1	4-1
Galway United FC	3-1	1-0	2-1	1-1	3-0		3-0	1-0	1-0	1-1	0-1	0-0
Kildare County FC	1-3	4-1	2-0	2-3	0-3	3-2		3-1	1-3	0-0	1-0	1-1
Kilkenny City FC	1-2	1-2	0-0	2-2	0-1	1-1	4-1		0-2	0-3	1-1	1-3
Limerick FC	0-0	2-3	1-3	1-2	2-5	1-1	0-0	1-3		1-0	3-2	1-3
Monaghan United FC	1-0	1-1	1-1	1-1	1-1	1-1	0-4	1-1	3-1		0-1	1-1
Sligo Rovers FC	3-0	3-2	1-1	0-2	1-1	4-2	0-0	1-0	0-0	0-2		1-2
Waterford United FC	2-2	2-0	2-1	1-0	0-0	1-0	2-2	4-0	1-0	2-2	1-0	

Promotion/Relegation Play-offs   (29/01/03 – 08/02/03)

Galway United FC (Galway)	2-0, 0-3	Drogheda United FC (Drogheda)
Cobh Ramblers FC (Cobh)	2-2, 0-2	Drogheda United FC (Drogheda)
Galway United FC (Galway)	2-0, 0-1	Finn Harps FC (Ballybofey)

	Division One	**Pd**	**Wn**	**Dw**	**Ls**	**GF**	**GA**	**Pts**	
1.	Waterford United FC (Waterford)	22	13	7	2	37	25	46	P
2.	Finn Harps FC (Ballybofey)	22	12	5	5	41	22	41	PO
3.	Galway United FC (Galway)	22	10	6	6	34	21	36	PO
4.	Cobh Ramblers FC (Cobh)	22	10	5	7	39	38	35	PO
5.	Kildare County FC (Newbridge)	22	9	6	7	32	31	33	
6.	Sligo Rovers FC (Sligo)	22	8	6	8	28	27	30	
7.	Dublin City FC (Dublin)	22	8	4	10	36	35	28	
8.	Monaghan United FC (Monaghan)	22	5	11	6	26	27	26	
9.	Dundalk FC (Dundalk)	22	5	8	9	28	36	23	
10	Limerick FC (Limerick)	22	6	5	11	26	36	23	
11.	Athlone Town AFC (Athlone)	22	5	6	11	26	40	21	
12.	Kilkenny City FC (Kilkenny)	22	3	7	12	23	38	16	
		264	94	76	94	376	376	358	

The season was changed to run from Spring to Autumn.

2003

League of Ireland Division One 2003	Athlone Town AFC	Bray Wanderers AFC	Cobh Ramblers FC	Dublin City FC	Dundalk FC	Finn Harps FC	Galway United FC	Kildare County FC	Kilkenny City FC	Limerick AFC	Monaghan United FC	Sligo Rovers FC
Athlone Town AFC (Athlone)	■	1-0	2-0	1-2		1-2						3-0
	■	2-0	0-1	0-1	0-1	1-2	0-0	2-3	2-1	2-0	1-0	1-1
Bray Wanderers AFC (Bray)		■	3-1		2-0	3-1			3-0		1-0	
	5-3	■	3-1	1-1	3-1	1-1	2-0	3-2	2-1	2-1	2-1	0-0
Cobh Ramblers FC (Cobh)			■			0-0	2-0	1-1	3-2	0-2		0-1
	2-0	1-2	■	1-3	2-1	1-0	0-5	1-2	0-0	0-2	6-1	1-1
Dublin City FC (Dublin)		1-1	0-0	■		1-0	1-0		2-2		2-1	
	1-1	1-1	0-0	■	1-0	0-3	2-0	0-1	2-1	3-1	1-1	1-0
Dundalk FC (Dundalk)	1-1		0-2		■	1-2		2-1		0-1		
	1-1	1-1	0-0	0-2	■	1-1	4-0	0-0	1-1	3-1	2-1	2-2
Finn Harps FC (Ballybofey)						■	3-1	2-1	1-0	0-1	2-0	0-1
	1-1	2-0	5-0	2-2	3-1	■	1-1	2-0	6-0	0-0	2-1	1-0
Galway United FC (Galway)	1-1	3-3		0-1	0-5		■					2-1
	2-2	2-2	1-0	2-2	1-1	2-2	■	0-1	4-1	4-3	4-1	1-1
Kildare County FC (Newbridge)	2-0	0-3				0-2		■			3-0	0-0
	1-1	0-1	3-1	1-0	3-2	0-0	5-3	■	1-0	1-1	3-1	2-1
Kilkenny City FC (Kilkenny)	0-1			0-1	0-0		0-1	2-3	■			1-2
	2-1	0-3	1-2	0-1	3-3	1-4	0-1	0-3	■	1-4	1-1	0-1
Limerick AFC (Limerick)	4-3	2-2		1-0			5-0	1-1	1-1	■	3-1	
	1-0	1-2	1-1	0-1	2-1	1-1	1-1	2-1	2-1	■	1-0	4-0
Monaghan United FC (Monaghan)	0-1		1-1		1-1		0-3		1-0		■	
	3-0	0-0	1-1	0-2	0-0	1-2	0-0	1-1	5-2	2-3	■	2-3
Sligo Rovers FC (Sligo)		3-2		2-3	1-0					1-1	3-1	■
	1-1	1-0	1-1	2-3	0-0	0-0	1-1	2-2	0-2	2-1	4-0	■

Promotion/Relegation Play-offs   (03/12/03 – 13/12/03)

Finn Harps FC (Ballybofey)	0-0, 1-2 (aet)	Derry City FC (Derry)
Finn Harps FC (Ballybofey)	1-0, 2-1	Bray Wanderers AFC (Bray)
Limerick FC (Limerick)	0-0, 0-4	Derry City FC (Derry)

	Division One	Pd	Wn	Dw	Ls	GF	GA	Pts	
1.	Dublin City FC (Dublin)	33	19	10	4	44	26	67	P
2.	Bray Wanderers AFC (Bray)	33	18	10	5	59	35	64	PO
3.	Finn harps FC (Ballybofey)	33	17	11	5	52	24	62	PO
4.	Limerick FC (Limerick)	33	16	9	8	55	38	57	PO
5.	Kildare County FC (Newbridge)	33	15	10	8	50	39	55	
6.	Sligo Rovers FC (Sligo)	33	11	13	9	39	39	46	
7.	Galway United FC (Galway)	33	10	13	10	48	53	43	
8.	Cobh Ramblers FC (Cobh)	33	9	11	13	33	45	38	
9.	Athlone Town AFC (Athlone)	33	9	10	14	37	42	37	
10	Dundalk FC (Dundalk)	33	6	14	13	36	40	32	
11.	Monaghan United FC (Monaghan)	33	3	9	21	28	60	15	*
12.	Kilkenny City FC (Kilkenny)	33	2	6	25	25	65	12	
		396	135	126	135	506	506	528	

* Monaghan United FC (Monaghan) had 3 points deducted for fielding an ineligible player in the Round 18 match versus Dublin City FC (which they lost 0-2).

2004

League of Ireland Division One 2004	Athlone Town AFC	Bray Wanderers AFC	Cobh Ramblers FC	Dundalk FC	Finn Harps FC	Galway United FC	Kildare County FC	Kilkenny City FC	Limerick FC	Monaghan United FC	Sligo Rovers FC	U.C. Dublin
Athlone Town AFC (Athlone)	■			1-4		1-2	1-2	2-1	1-1	0-1		
		0-2	3-2	0-2	1-2	1-0	1-2	2-0	4-0	4-1	2-2	0-1
Bray Wanderers AFC (Bray)	5-3	■				1-1	0-0		0-0		2-0	2-2
	2-1		3-0	5-1	0-0	1-0	1-1	3-1	2-0	4-2	4-0	0-2
Cobh Ramblers FC (Cobh)	1-0	1-2	■	2-1						5-0		0-1
	5-0	1-4		1-0	2-4	0-0	1-5	1-1	0-1	3-1	3-2	1-1
Dundalk FC (Dundalk)		3-2		■		1-1		3-1		1-2	3-2	1-3
	4-1	0-6	2-2		0-2	1-3	2-1	1-1	2-1	0-1	1-0	0-1
Finn Harps FC (Ballybofey)	6-0	2-0	1-0	3-0	■						1-0	0-1
	1-0	0-1	0-0	2-0		2-1	2-2	1-0	3-1	3-1	3-0	1-0
Galway United FC (Galway)			4-3		1-5	■	2-6	1-1	3-0	1-1		
	4-0	3-1	0-0	3-3	1-1		1-1	1-0	3-1	4-1	3-1	1-1
Kildare County FC (Newbridge)		2-0	2-0	0-2			■	3-1	2-0			1-2
	2-1	0-2	2-1	1-0	1-1	1-3		1-1	0-0	1-2	2-0	0-0
Kilkenny City FC (Kilkenny)		0-1	2-1	0-1				■	2-1	0-3		
	1-0	0-0	1-1	0-2	2-1	1-2	0-2		0-1	1-0	2-2	1-1
Limerick FC (Limerick)			1-3	1-2	1-4				■	1-1	1-0	
	1-2	1-0	1-1	1-2	1-2	0-3	0-2	0-0		0-0	0-1	0-3
Monaghan United FC (Monaghan)		1-4		0-0		0-1				■	1-0	0-0
	1-5	1-2	2-0	1-2	0-1	0-1	0-1	0-3	2-0		0-1	0-3
Sligo Rovers FC (Sligo)	1-2		1-1		3-1	3-1	4-2				■	
	2-0	0-0	2-2	2-0	1-2	3-1	2-3	4-1	1-0	4-0		1-2
University College Dublin AFC (Dublin)	3-0				3-0		3-0	1-1		2-0		■
	4-3	2-0	1-1	2-1	1-1	4-0	0-2	4-1	3-0	4-1	2-1	

	Division 1	Pd	Wn	Dw	Ls	GF	GA	Pts	
1.	Finn Harps FC (Ballybofey)	33	23	7	3	60	19	76	P
2.	University College Dublin AFC (Dublin)	33	22	9	2	63	21	75	P
3.	Bray Wanderers AFC (Bray)	33	19	8	6	62	29	65	P
4.	Kildare County FC (Newbridge)	33	18	8	7	54	32	62	
5.	Galway United FC (Galway)	33	14	10	9	55	49	52	
6.	Dundalk FC (Dundalk)	33	14	4	15	46	57	46	
7.	Sligo Rovers FC (Sligo)	33	11	5	17	46	50	38	
8.	Cobh Ramblers FC (Cobh)	33	7	11	15	47	53	32	
9.	Kilkenny City FC (Kilkenny)	33	6	9	18	28	53	27	
10.	Athlone Town AFC (Athlone)	33	9	2	22	42	68	26	*
11.	Monaghan United FC (Monaghan)	33	8	5	20	28	63	26	*
12.	Limerick FC (Limerick)	33	4	8	21	18	55	20	
		396	155	86	155	549	549	545	

* Athlone Town AFC (Athlone) and Monaghan United FC (Monaghan) each had 3 points deducted for fielding an ineligible player.

EIRCOM LEAGUE FIRST DIVISION FIXTURES 2005

SERIES Nº 1

Friday 18th March	Athlone Town vs Dundalk at St. Mel's Park	7.45pm
Saturday 19th March	Kilkenny City vs Dublin City at Buckley Park	7.30pm
Saturday 19th March	Sligo Rovers vs Kildare County at The Showgrounds	7.30pm
Saturday 19th March	Cobh Ramblers vs Limerick at St. Colman's Park	7.45pm
Sunday 20th March	Monaghan United vs Galway United Century at Homes Park	3.00pm

SERIES Nº 2

Thursday 24th March	Dublin City vs Sligo Rovers at Tolka Park	7.45pm
Thursday 24th March	Dundalk vs Kilkenny City at Oriel Park	7.45pm
Friday 25th March	Galway United vs Athlone Town at Terryland Park	7.30pm
Friday 25th March	Limerick vs Monaghan United at Hogan Park	7.45pm
Saturday 26th March	Kildare County vs Cobh Ramblers at Newbridge	7.30pm

SERIES Nº 3

Thursday 31st March	Dublin City vs Kildare County at Tolka Park	7.45pm
Friday 1st April	Athlone Town vs Limerick at St. Mel's Park	7.45pm
Saturday 2nd April	Kilkenny City vs Galway United at Buckley Park	7.30pm
Saturday 2nd April	Sligo Rovers vs Dundalk at The Showgrounds	7.30pm
Sunday 3rd April	Monaghan United vs Cobh Ramblers Century at Homes Park	3.00pm

MIDWEEK – SERIES Nº 4

TBC	Cobh Ramblers vs Athlone Town at St. Colman's Park	TBC
TBC	Dundalk vs Dublin City at Oriel Park	TBC
TBC	Galway United vs Sligo Rovers at Terryland Park	TBC
TBC	Kildare County vs Monaghan United at Newbridge	TBC
TBC	Limerick vs Kilkenny City at Hogan Park	TBC

SERIES Nº 5

Thursday 7th April	Dublin City vs Galway United at Tolka Park	7.45pm
Thursday 7th April	Dundalk vs Kildare County at Oriel Park	7.45pm
Friday 8th April	Athlone Town vs Monaghan United at St. Mel's Park	7.45pm
Saturday 9th April	Kilkenny City vs Cobh Ramblers at Buckley Park	7.30pm
Saturday 9th April	Sligo Rovers vs Limerick at The Showgrounds	7.30pm

SERIES Nº 6

Friday 15th April	Galway United vs Dundalk at Terryland Park	7.30pm
Friday 15th April	Limerick vs Dublin City at Hogan Park	7.45pm
Saturday 16th April	Kildare County vs Athlone Town at Newbridge	7.30pm
Saturday 16th April	Cobh Ramblers vs Sligo Rovers at St. Colman's Park	7.45pm
Sunday 17th April	Monaghan United vs Kilkenny City Century at Homes Park	3.00pm

SERIES No 7

Thursday 21st April	Dublin City vs Cobh Ramblers at Tolka Park	7.45pm
Thursday 21st April	Dundalk vs Limerick at Oriel Park	7.45pm
Friday 22nd April	Galway United vs Kildare County at Terryland Park	7.30pm
Saturday 23rd April	Kilkenny City vs Athlone Town at Buckley Park	7.30pm
Saturday 23rd April	Sligo Rovers vs Monaghan United at The Showgrounds	7.30pm

SERIES No 8

Friday 29th April	Athlone Town vs Sligo Rovers at St. Mel's Park	7.45pm
Friday 29th April	Limerick vs Galway United at Hogan Park	7.45pm
Saturday 30th April	Kilkenny City vs Kildare County at Buckley Park	7.30pm
Saturday 30th April	Cobh Ramblers vs Dundalk at St. Colman's Park	7.45pm
Sunday 1st May	Monaghan United vs Dublin City Century at Homes Park	3.00pm

SERIES No 9

Thursday 5th May	Dublin City vs Athlone Town at Tolka Park	7.45pm
Thursday 5th May	Dundalk vs Monaghan United at Oriel Park	7.45pm
Friday 6th May	Galway United vs Cobh Ramblers at Terryland Park	7.30pm
Saturday 7th May	Kildare County vs Limerick at Newbridge	7.30pm
Saturday 7th May	Sligo Rovers vs Kilkenny City at The Showgrounds	7.30pm

SERIES No 10

Thursday 12th May	Dublin City vs Kilkenny City at Tolka Park	7.45pm
Thursday 12th May	Dundalk vs Athlone Town at Oriel Park	7.45pm
Friday 13th May	Galway United vs Monaghan United at Terryland Park	7.30pm
Friday 13th May	Limerick vs Cobh Ramblers at Hogan Park	7.45pm
Saturday 14th May	Kildare County vs Sligo Rovers at Newbridge	7.30pm

SERIES No 11

Friday 20th May	Athlone Town vs Galway United at St. Mel's Park	7.45pm
Saturday 21st May	Kilkenny City vs Dundalk at Buckley Park	7.30pm
Saturday 21st May	Sligo Rovers vs Dublin City at The Showgrounds	7.30pm
Saturday 21st May	Cobh Ramblers vs Kildare County at St. Colman's Park	7.45pm
Sunday 22nd May	Monaghan United vs Limerick Century at Homes Park	3.00pm

SERIES No 12

Thursday 26th May	Dundalk vs Sligo Rovers at Oriel Park	7.45pm
Friday 27th May	Galway United vs Kilkenny City at Terryland Park	7.30pm
Friday 27th May	Limerick vs Athlone Town at Hogan Park	7.45pm
Saturday 28th May	Kildare County vs Dublin City at Newbridge	7.30pm
Saturday 28th May	Cobh Ramblers vs Monaghan United at St. Colman's Park	7.45pm

SERIES No 13th

Thursday 2nd June	Dublin City vs Dundalk at Tolka Park	7.45pm
Friday 3rd June	Athlone Town vs Cobh Ramblers at St. Mel's Park	7.45pm
Saturday 4th June	Kilkenny City vs Limerick at Buckley Park	7.30pm
Saturday 4th June	Sligo Rovers vs Galway United at The Showgrounds	7.30pm
Sunday 5th June	Monaghan United vs Kildare County Century at Homes Park	3.00pm

WEEKEND ENDING SUNDAY 12th JUNE — FAI CUP SECOND ROUND

SERIES No 14

Friday 17th June	Galway United vs Dublin City at Terryland Park	7.30pm
Friday 17th June	Limerick vs Sligo Rovers at Hogan Park	7.45pm
Saturday 18th June	Kildare County vs Dundalk at Newbridge	7.30pm
Saturday 18th June	Cobh Ramblers vs Kilkenny City at St. Colman's Park	7.45pm
Sunday 19th June	Monaghan United vs Athlone Town Century at Homes Park	3.00pm

SERIES No 15

Thursday 23rd June	Dublin City vs Limerick at Tolka Park	7.45pm
Thursday 23rd June	Dundalk vs Galway United at Oriel Park	7.45pm
Friday 24th June	Athlone Town vs Kildare County at St. Mel's Park	7.45pm
Saturday 25th June	Kilkenny City vs Monaghan United at Buckley Park	7.30pm
Saturday 25th June	Sligo Rovers vs Cobh Ramblers at The Showgrounds	7.30pm

SERIES No 16

Friday 1st July	Athlone Town vs Kilkenny City at St. Mel's Park	7.45pm
Friday 1st July	Limerick vs Dundalk at Hogan Park	7.45pm
Saturday 2nd July	Kildare County vs Galway United at Newbridge	7.30pm
Saturday 2nd July	Cobh Ramblers vs Dublin City at St. Colman's Park	7.45pm
Sunday 3rd July	Monaghan United vs Sligo Rovers Century at Homes Park	3.00pm

SERIES No 17

Thursday 7th July	Dublin City vs Monaghan United at Tolka Park	7.45pm
Thursday 7th July	Dundalk vs Cobh Ramblers at Oriel Park	7.45pm
Friday 8th July	Galway United vs Limerick at Terryland Park	7.30pm
Saturday 9th July	Kildare County vs Kilkenny City at Newbridge	7.30pm
Saturday 9th July	Sligo Rovers vs Athlone Town at The Showgrounds	7.30pm

SERIES No 18

Friday 15th July	Limerick vs Kildare County at Hogan Park	7.45pm
Friday 15th July	Athlone Town vs Dublin City at St. Mel's Park	7.45pm
Saturday 16th July	Kilkenny City vs Sligo Rovers at Buckley Park	7.30pm
Saturday 16th July	Cobh Ramblers vs Galway United at St. Colman's Park	7.45pm
Sunday 17th July	Monaghan United vs Dundalk Century at Homes Park	3.00pm

SERIES Nº 19

Friday 22nd July	Athlone Town vs Dundalk at St. Mel's Park	7.45pm
Saturday 23rd July	Kilkenny City vs Dublin City at Buckley Park	7.30pm
Saturday 23rd July	Sligo Rovers vs Kildare County at The Showgrounds	7.30pm
Saturday 23rd July	Cobh Ramblers vs Limerick at St. Colman's Park	7.45pm
Sunday 24th July	Monaghan United vs Galway United Century at Homes Park	3.00pm

SERIES Nº 20

Thursday 28th July	Dublin City vs Sligo Rovers at Tolka Park	7.45pm
Thursday 28th July	Dundalk vs Kilkenny City at Oriel Park	7.45pm
Friday 29th July	Galway United vs Athlone Town at Terryland Park	7.30pm
Friday 29th July	Limerick vs Monaghan United at Hogan Park	7.45pm
Saturday 30th July	Kildare County vs Cobh Ramblers at Newbridge	7.30pm

MIDWEEK – SERIES Nº 21

TBC	Athlone Town vs Limerick at St. Mel's Park	7.45pm
TBC	Dublin City vs Kildare County at Tolka Park	7.45pm
TBC	Kilkenny City vs Galway United at Buckley Park	7.45pm
TBC	Monaghan United vs Cobh Ramblers Century at Homes Park	3.00pm
TBC	Sligo Rovers vs Dundalk at The Showgrounds	7.30pm

SERIES Nº 22

Thursday 4th August	Dundalk vs Dublin City at Oriel Park	7.45pm
Friday 5th August	Galway United vs Sligo Rovers at Terryland Park	7.30pm
Friday 5th August	Limerick vs Kilkenny City at Hogan Park	7.45pm
Saturday 6th August	Kildare County vs Monaghan United at Buckley Park	7.30pm
Saturday 6th August	Cobh Ramblers vs Athlone Town at St. Colman's Park	7.45pm

SERIES Nº 23

Thursday 11th August	Dublin City vs Galway United at Tolka Park	7.45pm
Thursday 11th August	Dundalk vs Kildare County at Oriel Park	7.45pm
Friday 12th August	Athlone Town vs Monaghan United at St. Mel's Park	7.45pm
Saturday 13th August	Kilkenny City vs Cobh Ramblers at Buckley Park	7.30pm
Saturday 13th August	Sligo Rovers vs Limerick at The Showgrounds	7.30pm

SERIES Nº 24

Friday 19th August	Galway United vs Dundalk at Terryland Park	7.30pm
Friday 19th August	Limerick vs Dublin City at Hogan Park	7.45pm
Saturday 20th August	Kildare County vs Athlone Town at Newbridge	7.30pm
Saturday 20th August	Cobh Ramblers vs Sligo Rovers at St. Colman's Park	7.45pm
Sunday 21st August	Monaghan United vs Kilkenny City Century at Homes Park	3.00pm

WEEKEND ENDING SUNDAY 28th AUGUST — FAI CUP THIRD ROUND

SERIES N⁰ 25

Thursday 1st September	Dublin City vs Cobh Ramblers at Tolka Park	7.45pm
Thursday 1st September	Dundalk vs Limerick at Oriel Park	7.45pm
Friday 2nd September	Galway United vs Kildare County at Terryland Park	7.30pm
Saturday 3rd September	Kilkenny City vs Athlone Town at Buckley Park	7.30pm
Saturday 3rd September	Sligo Rovers vs Monaghan United at The Showgrounds	7.30pm

SERIES N⁰ 26

Friday 9th September	Athlone Town vs Sligo Rovers at St. Mel's Park	7.45pm
Friday 9th September	Limerick vs Galway United at Hogan Park	7.45pm
Saturday 10th September	Kilkenny City vs Kildare County at Buckley Park	7.30pm
Saturday 10th September	Cobh Ramblers vs Dundalk at St. Colman's Park	7.45pm
Sunday 11th September	Monaghan United vs Dublin City Century at Homes Park	3.00pm

SERIES N⁰ 27

Thursday 15th September	Dundalk vs Monaghan United at Oriel Park	7.45pm
Thursday 15th September	Dublin City vs Athlone Town at Tolka Park	7.45pm
Friday 16th September	Galway United vs Cobh Ramblers at Terryland Park	7.30pm
Saturday 17th September	Kildare County vs Limerick at Buckley Park	7.30pm
Saturday 17th September	Sligo Rovers vs Kilkenny City at The Showgrounds	7.30pm

SERIES N⁰ 28 AND FAI CUP QUARTER-FINALS

Thursday 22nd September	Dublin City vs Kilkenny City at Tolka Park	7.45pm
Thursday 22nd September	Dundalk vs Athlone Town at Oriel Park	7.45pm
Friday 23rd September	Galway United vs Monaghan United at Terryland Park	7.30pm
Friday 23rd September	Limerick vs Cobh Ramblers at Hogan Park	7.45pm
Saturday 24th September	Kildare County vs Sligo Rovers at Newbridge	7.30pm

SERIES N⁰ 29

Friday 30th September	Athlone Town vs Galway United at St. Mel's Park	7.45pm
Saturday 1st October	Kilkenny City vs Dundalk at Buckley Park	7.30pm
Saturday 1st October	Sligo Rovers vs Dublin City at The Showgrounds	7.30pm
Saturday 1st October	Cobh Ramblers vs Kildare County at St. Colman's Park	7.45pm
Sunday 2nd October	Monaghan United vs Limerick Century at Homes Park 3.00pm	

SERIES N⁰ 30th

Thursday 6th October	Dundalk vs Sligo Rovers at Oriel Park	7.45pm
Friday 7th October	Galway United vs Kilkenny City at Terryland Park	7.30pm
Friday 7th October	Limerick vs Athlone Town at Hogan Park	7.45pm
Saturday 8th October	Kildare County vs Dublin City at Buckley Park	7.30pm
Saturday 8th October	Cobh Ramblers vs Monaghan United at St. Colman's Park	7.45pm

SERIES Nº 31

Thursday 13th October	Dublin City vs Dundalk at Tolka Park	7.45pm
Friday 14th October	Athlone Town vs Cobh Ramblers at St. Mel's Park	7.45pm
Saturday 15th October	Kilkenny City vs Limerick at Buckley Park	7.30pm
Saturday 15th October	Sligo Rovers vs Galway United at The Showgrounds	7.30pm
Sunday 16th October	Monaghan United vs Kildare County Century at Homes Park	3.00pm

SERIES Nº 32 AND FAI CUP SEMI-FINALS

Friday 21st October	Galway United vs Dublin City at Terryland Park	7.30pm
Friday 21st October	Limerick vs Sligo Rovers at Hogan Park	7.45pm
Saturday 22nd October	Kildare County vs Dundalk at Newbridge	7.30pm
Saturday 22nd October	Cobh Ramblers vs Kilkenny City at St. Colman's Park	7.45pm
Sunday 23rd October	Monaghan United vs Athlone Town Century at Homes Park	3.00pm

SERIES Nº 33

Thursday 27th October	Dublin City vs Limerick at Tolka Park	7.45pm
Thursday 27th October	Dundalk vs Galway United at Oriel Park	7.45pm
Friday 28th October	Athlone Town vs Kildare County at St. Mel's Park	7.45pm
Saturday 29th October	Kilkenny City vs Monaghan United at Buckley Park	7.30pm
Saturday 29th October	Sligo Rovers vs Cobh Ramblers at The Showgrounds	7.30pm

SERIES Nº 34

Friday 4th November	Athlone Town vs Kilkenny City at St. Mel's Park	7.45pm
Friday 4th November	Limerick vs Dundalk at Hogan Park	7.45pm
Saturday 5th November	Kildare County vs Galway United at Newbridge	7.30pm
Saturday 5th November	Cobh Ramblers vs Dublin City at St. Colman's Park	7.45pm
Sunday 6th November	Monaghan United vs Sligo Rovers Century at Homes Park	3.00pm

SERIES Nº 35

Thursday 10th November	Dublin City vs Monaghan United at Tolka Park	7.45pm
Thursday 10th November	Dundalk vs Cobh Ramblers at Oriel Park	7.45pm
Friday 11th November	Galway United vs Limerick at Terryland Park	7.30pm
Saturday 12th November	Kildare County vs Kilkenny City at Newbridge	7.30pm
Saturday 12th November	Sligo Rovers vs Athlone Town at The Showgrounds	7.30pm

SERIES Nº 36

Friday 18th November	Limerick vs Kildare County at Hogan Park	7.45pm
Friday 18th November	Athlone Town vs Dublin City at St. Mel's Park	7.45pm
Saturday 19th November	Kilkenny City vs Sligo Rovers at Buckley Park	7.30pm
Saturday 19th November	Cobh Ramblers vs Galway United at St. Colman's Park	7.45pm
Sunday 20th November	Monaghan United vs Dundalk Century at Homes Park	3.00pm

1995-96

FAI Cup Final (Lansdowne Road, Dublin – 06/05/96)

SHELBOURNE FC (DUBLIN)   1-1   St. Patrick's Athletic FC (Dublin)
Sheridan 86'   *Campbell 76'*

Shelbourne: Gough, Costello, Neville, Duffy (Rutherford 82'), D.Geoghegan, Sheridan, Kelly (McKop 66'), Flood, O'Rourke, Tilson, S.Geoghegan.

St, Patrick's Athletic: Byrne, Burke, McDonnell, D.Campbell, Carpenter, P.Campbell, Menagh, Gormley, Osam, O'Flaherty (Glynn 79'), Buckley (Reilly 69').

FAI Cup Final Replay (Lansdowne Road, Dublin – 13/05/96)

SHELBOURNE FC (DUBLIN)   2-1   St. Patrick's Athletic FC (Dublin)
Sheridan 71', Geoghegan 82'   *Campbell 63'*

St. Patrick's Athletic: Byrne, Burke, McDonnell (P.Campbell 30'), D.Campbell, Carpenter, Osam (Reilly 45'), Menagh (Glynn 82'), Gormley, Buckley, Morris-Roe, O'Flaherty.

Shelbourne: Gough, Costello, Neville, Duffy, D.Geoghegan, Sheridan, Kelly (Rutherford 64'), Flood, O'Rourke, Tilson, S.Geoghegan.

Semi-Finals

Bohemian FC (Dublin)	0-0, 0-0 (aet), 1-2	St. Patrick's Athletic FC (Dublin)
Sligo Rovers FC (Sligo)	0-1	Shelbourne FC (Dublin)

Quarter-Finals

Cork City FC (Cork)	1-2	Sligo Rovers FC (Sligo)
Derry City FC (Derry)	0-3	Shelbourne FC (Dublin)
Finn Harps FC (Ballybofey)	0-0, 0-2	Bohemian FC (Dublin)
Wayside Celtic FC (Dublin)	0-3	St. Patrick's Athletic FC (Dublin)

Round 2

Bohemian FC (Dublin)	4-0	Kilkenny City FC (Kilkenny)
Derry City FC (Derry)	2-0	Avondale United FC (Cork)
Drogheda United FC (Drogheda)	0-2	Shelbourne FC (Dublin)
Finn Harps FC (Ballybofey)	1-1, 4-1	Athlone Town AFC (Athlone)
Home Farm-Everton FC (Dublin)	1-1, 0-1	Cork City FC (Cork)
Limerick FC (Limerick)	1-3	Sligo Rovers FC (Sligo)
St. Patrick's Athletic FC (Dublin)	3-0	Fanad United FC (Ballylar)
Waterford United FC (Waterford)	0-0, 1-1, 1-2	Wayside Celtic FC (Dublin)

Round 1

Athlone Town AFC (Athlone)	2-1	Monaghan United FC (Monaghan)
Avondale United FC (Cork)	3-1	C.Y.M. Terenure (Dublin)
Bohemian FC (Dublin)	2-0	Moyle Park College AFC (Dublin)
Bray Wanderers AFC (Bray)	0-4	Fanad United FC (Ballylar)
Cobh Ramblers FC (Cobh)	1-2	Sligo Rovers FC (Sligo)
Derry City FC (Derry)	0-0, 1-0	St. James's Gate AFC (Dublin)
Dundalk FC (Dundalk)	1-1 (aet), 1-2	Drogheda United FC (Drogheda)
Finn Harps FC (Ballybofey)	5-2	Longford Town FC (Longford)
St. Patrick's Athletic FC (Dublin)	3-1	Workmans'/Dunleary FC (Dun Laoghaire)
Shamrock Rovers FC (Dublin)	0-0, 0-1	Shelbourne FC (Dublin)
T.E.K. United FC (Dublin)	0-1	Cork City FC (Cork)
Temple United FC (Cork)	2-3	Home Farm-Everton FC (Dublin)

U.C.C.	0-1	Limerick FC Limerick)
University College Dublin AFC (Dublin)	1-2	Kilkenny City FC (Kilkenny)
Waterford United FC (Waterford)	3-2	Galway United FC (Galway)
Wayside Celtic FC (Dublin)	2-1	Cherry Orchard FC (Dublin)

1996-97

FAI Cup Final   (Dalymount Park, Dublin – 04/05/97)

SHELBOURNE FC (DUBLIN)	2-0	Derry City FC (Derry)

Campbell 81', S.Geoghegan 87'

Shelbourne: Gough, Neville, Campbell, Scully, D.Geoghegan, Vaudequin (Costello 88'), Sheridan, Flood, O'Rourke, Rutherford (Baker 89'), S.Geoghegan.

Derry City: Devine, Boyle (Semple 83'), Dyles, Curran, Dunne, Hargan Hutton, Hegarty, Keddy, Beckett, L.Coyle.

Semi-Finals

Bohemian FC (Dublin)	0-2	Derry City FC (Derry)
Waterford United FC (Waterford)	1-2	Shelbourne FC (Dublin)

Quarter-Finals

Bohemian FC (Dublin)	1-0	St. Patrick's Athletic FC (Dublin)
Bray Wanderers AFC (Bray)	0-1	Shelbourne FC (Dublin)
Derry City FC (Derry)	1-0	Cork City FC (Cork)
Waterford United FC (Waterford)	1-0	Drogheda United FC (Drogheda)

Round 2

Bohemian FC (Dublin)	2-0	Wayside Celtic FC (Dublin)
Cork City FC (Cork)	4-1	St. Francis FC (Dublin)
Derry City FC (Derry)	2-1	Home Farm-Everton FC (Dublin)
Drogheda United FC (Drogheda)	2-1	Rockmount FC (Whitechurch)
Dublin University AFC (Dublin)	0-3	Bray Wanderers AFC (Bray)
Shelbourne FC (Dublin)	4-2	Dundalk FC (Dundalk)
Sligo Rovers FC (Sligo)	0-1	St. Patrick's Athletic FC (Dublin)
Waterford United FC (Waterford)	1-0	Shamrock Rovers FC (Dublin)

Round 1

Cobh Ramblers FC (Cobh)	0-3	Sligo Rovers FC (Sligo)
Cork City FC (Cork)	2-0	Galway United FC (Galway)
Derry City FC (Derry)	5-0	Crumlin United FC (Dublin)
Dublin University AFC (Dublin)	4-0	Parkvilla FC (Navan)
Garda AFC (Dublin)	0-2 (aet)	Drogheda United FC (Drogheda)
Home Farm-Everton FC (Dublin)	2-1	Glenmore Celtic FC (Dublin)
Kilkenny City FC (Kilkenny)	1-2	Bohemian FC (Dublin)
Longford Town FC (Longford)	0-1	St. Francis FC (Dublin)
St. Patrick's Athletic FC (Dublin)	1-0	Athlone Town AFC (Athlone)
Shamrock Rovers FC (Dublin)	5-4 (aet)	Limerick FC (Limerick)
Shelbourne FC (Dublin)	4-2	Everton AFC (Cork)
University College Dublin AFC (Dublin)	0-1	Bray Wanderers AFC (Bray)
Valeview Shankhill FC (Dublin)	0-1	Rockmount FC (Whitechurch)
Waterford United FC (Waterford)	4-0	Monaghan United FC (Monaghan)
Wayside Celtic FC (Dublin)	2-1	Finn Harps FC (Ballybofey)
Whitehall Rangers FC (Dublin)	0-0 (aet), 1-5	Dundalk FC (Dundalk)

1997-98

FAI Cup Final   (Dalymount Park, Dublin – 10/05/98)

CORK CITY FC (CORK)   0-0   Shelbourne FC (Dublin)

Cork City: Mooney, Napier, Coughlan, Daly, Cronin, Flanagan, Freyne, Hill, Cahill, Glynn, Kabia (Caulfield 60').

Shelbourne: Gough, Costello (Smith 46'), McCarthy, Scully, D.Geoghegan, Baker, Fenlon, Fitzgerald, Rutherford, S.Geoghegan, Kelly.

FAI Cup Final Replay   (Dalymount Park, Dublin – 16/05/98)

CORK CITY FC (CORK)   1-0   Shelbourne FC (Dublin)

Coughlan 75'

Shelbourne: Gough, Smith, Scully, McCarthy, D.Geoghegan, Kelly, Fitzgerald (Neville 85'), Fenlon, Rutherford (Sheridan 80'), Baker, S.Geoghegan (Morley 80').

Cork City: Mooney, O'Donoghue (Long 76'), Daly, Coughlan, Cronin, Hill, Flanagan, Freyne, Cahill, Caulfield, Hartigan (Glynn 55').

Semi-Finals

Athlone Town AFC (Athlone)	1-3	Cork City FC (Cork)
Finn harps FC (Ballybofey)	0-0, 0-1	Shelbourne FC (Dublin)

Quarter-Finals

Athlone Town AFC (Athlone)	1-1, 2-1	Longford Town FC (Longford)
Cork City FC (Cork)	2-0	Sligo Rovers FC (Sligo)
St. Patrick's Athletic FC (Dublin)	2-2, 1-1 (aet), 2-2 (aet)	Shelbourne FC (Dublin)
	(Shelbourne FC won 5-3 on penalties)	
University College Dublin AFC (Dublin)	0-1	Finn Harps FC (Ballybofey)

Round 2

Athlone Town AFC (Athlone)	2-1	Shamrock Rovers FC (Dublin)
Cobh Ramblers FC (Cobh)	1-3	St. Patrick's Athletic FC (Dublin)
Cork City FC (Cork)	1-1, 1-0	Derry City FC (Derry)
Dundalk FC (Dundalk)	0-0, 0-2	Shelbourne FC (Dublin)
Galway United FC (Galway)	2-2, 1-3	Finn Harps FC (Ballybofey)
Longford Town FC (Longford)	1-0	Whitehall Rangers FC (Dublin)
Sligo Rovers FC (Sligo)	2-0	St. Francis FC (Dublin)
University College Dublin AFC (Dublin)	1-1, 1-0	Home Farm-Everton FC (Dublin)

Round 1

Athlone Town AFC (Athlone)	3-0	College Corinthians AFC (Cork)
Bohemian FC (Dublin)	0-1	Cork City FC (Cork)
Cobh Wanderers FC (Cobh)	0-2	Galway United FC (Galway)
Derry City FC (Derry)	7-0	Rockmount FC (Whitechurch)
Drogheda United FC (Drogheda)	1-1, 0-2	Shamrock Rovers FC (Dublin)
Dundalk FC (Dundalk)	5-0	Swilly Rovers FC (Letterkenny)
Fanad United FC (Ballylar)	0-3	Whitehall Rangers FC (Dublin)
Finn Harps FC (Ballybofey)	2-0	Bray Wanderers AFC (Bray)
Home Farm-Everton FC (Dublin)	3-1	Home Farm FC (Dublin)
Kilkenny City FC (Kilkenny)	0-4	University College Dublin AFC (Dublin)
Monaghan United FC (Monaghan)	0-3	Cobh Ramblers FC (Cobh)
St. Francis FC (Dublin)	1-0	Cherry Orchard FC (Dublin)
Shelbourne FC (Dublin)	4-1	Limerick FC (Limerick)
Sligo Rovers FC (Sligo)	1-1, 2-0	Mervue United FC (Galway)
Waterford United FC (Waterford)	2-2, 0-3	St. Patrick's Athletic FC (Dublin)
Wayside Celtic FC (Dublin)	0-0, 1-1, 0-1	Longford Town FC (Longford)

1998-99

FAI Cup Final   (Tolka Park, Dublin – 10/05/99)

BRAY WANDERERS AFC (BRAY)   0-0   Finn Harps FC (Ballybofey)

Bray Wanderers: Walsh, Doohan, Tresson, Lynch, Kenny, Tierney, Smyth, Farrell, Ryan (Brien 28'), Fox, Keogh.

Finn Harps: McKenna, Scanlon, D.Boyle, Dykes, Minnock, Mohan, Harkin, O'Brien, Kavanagh, Speak, Mulligan.

FAI Cup Final Replay   (Tolka Park, Dublin – 16/05/99)

BRAY WANDERERS AFC (BRAY)   2-2   Finn Harps FC (Ballybofey)

O'Connor 87', O'Brien 120'   *Speak 60', Mohan 103'*

Finn Harps: McKenna, Scanlon, D.Boyle, Dykes, Minnock, Mohan (McGettigan 115'), O'Brien, Harkin (Bradley 108'), McGrenaghan, Speak (Sheridan 112'), Mulligan.

Bray Wanderers: Walsh, Lynch, Tresson, Doohan, Kenny, Tierney (Brien 27'), Smyth (Byrne 68'), Keogh, Farrell (O'Connor 40'), Fox, O'Brien.

FAI Cup Final 2nd Replay   (Tolka Park, Dublin – 20/05/99)

BRAY WANDERERS AFC (BRAY)   2-1   Finn Harps FC (Ballybofey)

Byrne 38', 73'   *Speak 12'*

Bray Wanderers: Walsh, Kenny, Doohan, Lynch, Farrell (Smyth 87'), O'Connor, Tresson, Fox, Keogh, Byrne, O'Brien.

Finn Harps: McKenna, Scanlon (R.Boyle 65'), D.Boyle, Dykes, Minnock, Mohan (Bradley 83'), O'Brien, Harkin, McGrenaghan (Sheridan 77'), Mulligan, Speak.

Semi-Finals

Galway United FC (Galway)	1-2	Finn Harps FC (Ballybofey)
Shelbourne FC (Dublin)	1-2	Bray Wanderers AFC (Bray)

Quarter-Finals

Derry City FC (Derry)	0-2	Shelbourne FC (Dublin)
Galway United FC (Galway)	1-0	St. Patrick's Athletic FC (Dublin)
Kilkenny City FC (Kilkenny)	2-2, -:+	Finn Harps FC (Ballybofey)

(Kilkenny forfeited the game after they refused to travel for the replay as they had only 2 fit players, both goalkeepers)

Sligo Rovers FC (Sligo)	1-1, 0-0, 0-1	Bray Wanderers AFC (Bray)

Round 2

Bohemian FC (Dublin)	0-1	Shelbourne FC (Dublin)
Bray Wanderers AFC (Bray)	3-0	Cherry Orchard FC (Dublin)
Cork City FC (Cork)	0-0, 0-1	Finn Harps FC (Ballybofey)
Derry City FC (Derry)	2-0	Dundalk FC (Dundalk)
Galway United FC (Galway)	1-0	Home Farm-Everton FC (Dublin)
St. Mary's FC (Cork)	0-3	Kilkenny City FC (Kilkenny)
St. Patrick's Athletic FC (Dublin)	1-0	University College Dublin AFC (Dublin)
Sligo Rovers FC (Sligo)	2-1	Cobh Ramblers FC (Cobh)

Round 1

Ashtown Villa FC (Dublin)	0-2	Cherry Orchard FC (Dublin)
Athlone Town AFC (Athlone)	0-1	Sligo Rovers FC (Sligo)
Bray Wanderers AFC (Bray)	5-0	St. Francis FC (Dublin)
Cobh Ramblers FC (Cobh)	2-2, 6-1	Garda AFC (Dublin)
Drogheda United FC (Drogheda)	0-0, 0-1	Galway United FC (Galway)
Finn Harps FC (Ballybofey)	0-0, 6-0	Belgrove FC (Dublin)
Glenmore Celtic FC (Dublin)	0-3	St. Patrick's Athletic FC (Dublin)
Kilkenny City FC (Kilkenny)	3-2	Swilly Rovers FC (Letterkenny)
Limerick FC (Limerick)	0-0, 2-2, 0-1	Dundalk FC (Dundalk)
Longford Town FC (Longford)	0-1	Derry City FC (Derry)
Monaghan United FC (Monaghan)	0-2	Cork City FC (Cork)
Rockmount FC (Whitechurch)	1-1, 0-2	University College Dublin AFC (Dublin)
St. Mary's FC (Cork)	1-0	Bangor Celtic FC
Shamrock Rovers FC (Dublin)	0-3	Shelbourne FC (Dublin)
Waterford United FC (Waterford)	0-4	Bohemian FC (Dublin)
Workmans'/Dunleary (Dun Laoghaire)	1-3	Home Farm-Everton FC (Dublin)

1999-2000

FAI Cup Final   (Tolka Park, Dublin – 30/04/00)

SHELBOURNE FC (DUBLIN)	0-0	Bohemian FC (Dublin)

Shelbourne: Williams, Heary, D.Geoghegan, McCarthy, Scully, D.Baker, Doolin, S.Geoghegan, Fenlon, Keddy, R.Baker.

Bohemian: Michael Dempsey, T.O'Connor, Brunton, Hunt (Doyle 61'), Maher, John, Byrne (Kelly 56'), Caffrey, Swan (Crowe 82'), G.O'Connor, Mark Dempsey.

FAI Cup Final Replay   (Dalymount Park, Dublin – 05/05/00 – 7,155)

SHELBOURNE FC (DUBLIN)	1-0	Bohemian FC (Dublin)

Fenlon 39'

Bohemian: Michael Dempsey, T.O'Connor, Brunton (Doyle 87'), Hunt, Maher, John, Byrne (Swan 51'), Caffrey, Kelly (Crowe 63'), G.O'Connor, Mark Dempsey.

Shelbourne: Williams, Heary, D.Geoghegan, McCarthy, Scully, D.Baker, Doolin (Campbell 90'), S.Geoghegan, Fenlon, Keddy, R.Baker.

Semi-Finals

Bohemian FC (Dublin)	2-1	Bray Wanderers AFC (Bray)
Galway United FC (Galway)	0-2	Shelbourne FC (Dublin)

Quarter-Finals

Bluebell United FC (Dublin)	0-0, 1-2	Shelbourne FC (Dublin)
Bohemian FC (Dublin)	2-0	St. Mochta's FC (Dublin)
Finn Harps FC (Ballybofey)	1-3	Galway United FC (Galway)
Kilkenny City FC (Kilkenny)	0-2	Bray Wanderers AFC (Bray)

Round 2

Athlone Town AFC (Athlone)	0-0, 1-1 (aet)	Galway United FC (Galway)
	(Galway United FC won 4-2 on penalties)	
Bangor Celtic FC	2-3	Shelbourne FC (Dublin)
Bohemian FC (Dublin)	3-3, 3-0	University College Dublin AFC (Dublin)
Clonmel Town FC (Clonmel)	1-1, 0-2	Bluebell United FC (Dublin)
Cork City FC (Cork)	0-2	Kilkenny City FC (Kilkenny)
Fairview Rangers FC (Limerick)	0-2	Bray Wanderers AFC (Bray)
Longford Town FC (Longford)	2-2, 1-7	Finn Harps FC (Ballybofey)
Swilly Rovers FC (Letterkenny)	1-2	St. Mochta's FC (Dublin)

Round 1

Athlone Town AFC (Athlone)	4-1	Limerick FC (Limerick)
Clonmel Town FC (Clonmel)	1-1, 3-1	Rockmount FC (Whitechurch)
Cobh Ramblers FC (Cobh)	0-1	Bohemians FC (Dublin)
Derry City FC (Derry)	1-1, 1-2	Bray Wanderers AFC (Bray)
Drogheda United FC (Drogheda)	0-1	Bangor Celtic FC
Fairview Rangers FC (Limerick)	0-0, 3-1 (aet)	College Corinthians AFC (Cork)
Finn Harps FC (Ballybofey)	2-0	Home Farm-Fingal FC (Dublin)
Galway United FC (Galway)	1-1, 3-2 (aet)	St. Patrick's Athletic FC (Dublin)
Kilkenny City FC (Kilkenny)	1-1, 1-1 (aet)	Dundalk FC (Dundalk)
	(Kilkenny City FC won 3-2 on penalties)	
Longford Town FC (Longford)	2-2, 1-0	Waterford United FC (Waterford)
Monaghan United FC (Monaghan)	0-4	University College Dublin AFC (Dublin)
St. Francis FC (Dublin)	0-1	Shelbourne FC (Dublin)
St. Mochta's FC (Dublin)	3-1	Evergreen FC
Shamrock Rovers FC (Dublin)	1-1, 1-3	Cork City FC (Cork)
Sligo Rovers FC (Sligo)	0-1	Bluebell United FC (Dublin)
Swilly Rovers FC (Letterkenny)	5-0	Parkvilla FC (Navan)

2000-01

FAI Cup Final   (Tolka Park, Dublin – 13/05/01 – 9,500)

BOHEMIAN FC (DUBLIN)	1-0	Longford Town FC (Longford)

O'Connor 62'

Bohemian: Russell, O'Connor, Hill, Caffrey, Maher, Moloy, Fullam (Webb 26'), Hunt, Rutherfrod, Nesovic (Morrison 48'), Crowe.

Longford Town: O'Brien, Murphy, Smith (Perth 88'), McNally, W.Byrne, Gavin (Holt 59'), S.Byrne, Kelly, Prunty, O'Connor, Zeller (Notaro 46').

Semi-Finals

Bohemian FC (Dublin)	1-0	Shamrock Rovers FC (Dublin)
Waterford United FC (Waterford)	1-1, 0-1	Longford Town FC (Longford)

Quarter-Finals

Cobh Ramblers FC (Cobh)	0-1	Waterford United FC (Waterford)
Kilkenny City FC (Kilkenny)	2-7	Bohemian FC (Dublin)
Portmarnock FC (Portmarnock)	1-2	Longford Town FC (Longford)
Shelbourne FC (Dublin)	1-1, 0-3	Shamrock Rovers FC (Dublin)

Round 2

Bohemian FC (Dublin)	2-1	Bray Wanderers AFC (Bray)
Cherry Orchard FC (Dublin)	1-1, 0-1	Kilkenny City FC (Kilkenny)
Cobh Ramblers FC (Cobh)	1-1, 1-0	Athlone Town AFC (Athlone)
Derry City FC (Derry)	1-1, 0-1	Shelbourne FC (Dublin)
Finn Harps FC (Ballybofey)	0-3	Shamrock Rovers FC (Dublin)
Longford Town FC (Longford)	0-0, 2-1	St. Patrick's Athletic FC (Dublin)
Portmarnock FC (Portmarnock)	1-0	Dundalk FC (Dundalk)
University College Dublin AFC (Dublin)	2-2, 0-0	Waterford United FC (Waterford)

Round 1

Bohemian FC (Dublin)	2-0	Drogheda United FC (Drogheda)
Bray Wanderers AFC (Bray)	5-0	Sligo Rovers FC (Sligo)
Cobh Ramblers FC (Cobh)	4-0	St. Michael's FC (Tipperary)
Dundalk FC (Dundalk)	3-0	Limerick FC (Limerick)
Galway United FC (Galway)	0-2	Kilkenny City FC (Kilkenny)
Home Farm FC (Dublin)	0-3	Finn Harps FC (Ballybofey)
Home Farm-Fingal (Dublin)	0-0, 0-1 (aet)	Athlone Town AFC (Athlone)
Longford Town FC (Longford)	1-1, 2-1	Cork City FC (Cork)
Moyle Park College AFC (Dublin)	0-1	Cherry Orchard FC (Dublin)
Portmarnock FC (Portmarnock)	3-0	Rockmount FC (Whitechurch)
Rathcoole Boys AFC	0-3	Derry City FC (Derry)
St. Patrick's Athletic FC (Dublin)	4-1	Wayside Celtic FC (Dublin)
Shamrock Rovers FC (Dublin)	3-0	Dublin Bus AFC (Dublin)
Shelbourne FC (Dublin)	2-0	Monaghan United FC (Monaghan)
University College Dublin AFC (Dublin)	3-1	Youghal United FC (Youghal)
Waterford United FC (Waterford)	1-1, 2-0	St. Francis FC (Dublin)

2001-02

FAI Cup Final   (Tolka Park, Dublin – 07/04/02)

DUNDALK FC (DUNDALK)	2-1	Bohemian FC (Dublin)

Haylock 44', 50'   *O'Connor 40'*

Dundalk: Connolly, Whyte, McGuinness, Broughan, Crawley, Hoey, Flanagan, Kavanagh, Lawless (McArdle 72'), Reilly, Haylock.

Bohemian: Russell, O'Connor, Caffrey, Hawkins, Webb, Harkin (Byrne 79'), Hunt, Morrison (Hill 72'), Rutherford, Molloy (O'Neill 86'), Crowe.

Semi-Finals

Bohemian FC (Dublin)	2-1	Derry City FC (Derry)
Dundalk FC (Dundalk)	4-0	Shamrock Rovers FC (Dublin)

Quarter-Finals

Bohemian FC (Dublin)	1-1, 4-0	Bray Wanderers AFC (Bray)
Dundalk FC (Dundalk)	1-1, 2-0	Finn Harps FC (Ballybofey)
Shamrock Rovers FC (Dublin)	2-0	Sligo Rovers FC (Sligo)
University College Dublin AFC (Dublin)	2-2, 0-1	Derry City FC (Derry)

Round 2

Bohemian FC (Dublin)	2-0	Cobh Ramblers FC (Cobh)
Cherry Orchard FC (Dublin)	0-3	University College Dublin AFC (Dublin)
Dublin City FC (Dublin)	0-2	Bray Wanderers AFC (Bray)
Finn Harps FC (Ballybofey)	2-1	Shelbourne FC (Dublin)
Kilkenny City FC (Kilkenny)	2-3	Dundalk FC (Dundalk)
St. Kevin's Boys AFC	0-0, 0-1	Derry City FC (Derry)
Shamrock Rovers FC (Dublin)	4-1	Monaghan United FC (Monaghan)
Sligo Rovers FC (Sligo)	2-1	Limerick FC (Limerick)

Round 1

Cherry Orchard FC (Dublin)	2-0	Garda AFC (Dublin)
Cork City FC (Cork)	0-1	Shamrock Rovers FC (Dublin)
C.Y.M. Terenure FC (Dublin)	0-1	Cobh Ramblers FC (Cobh)
Derry City FC (Derry)	2-0	Mervue United FC (Galway)
Drogheda United FC (Drogheda)	1-1, 0-2	University College Dublin AFC (Dublin)
Dundalk FC (Dundalk)	1-1, 1-0	Galway United FC (Galway)
Finn Harps FC (Ballybofey)	5-1	Greystones AFC (Greystones)
Glebe North FC (Balbriggan)	1-2	Limerick FC (Limerick)
Glenmore Dundrum FC (Dublin)	0-0, 1-5	Dublin City FC (Dublin)
Kilkenny City FC (Kilkenny)	2-1	Waterford United FC (Waterford)
Longford Town FC (Longford)	1-4	Bohemian FC (Dublin)
Monaghan United FC (Monaghan)	2-1	Athlone Town AFC (Athlone)
St. Kevin's Boys AFC	1-1, 3-2	Rockmount FC (Whitechurch)
St. Patrick's Athletic FC (Dublin)	0-1	Bray Wanderers AFC (Bray)
Sligo Rovers FC (Sligo)	2-0	Leeds AFC (Cork)
Workmans'/Dunleary (Dun Laoghaire)	0-3	Shelbourne FC (Dublin)

2002-03

FAI Cup Final   (Tolka Park, Dublin – 27/10/02 – 9,000)

DERRY CITY FC (DERRY)	1-0	Shamrock Rovers FC (Dublin)

Coyle 47'

Derry City: Gough, Harkin, McLaughlin, E.McCallion, Hargan, Hutton, Martyn, Doherty, Friars (McCready 66'), Coyle (T.McCallion 57'), Kelly.

Shamrock Rovers: O'Dowd, Costello, Scully, Palmer, Byrne (Robinson 69'), S.Grant (Francis 73'), Colwell, Dimech, Keddy, Hunt, T.Grant.

Semi-Finals

Cork City FC (Cork)	0-1	Derry City FC (Derry)
Shamrock Rovers FC (Dublin)	2-0	Bohemian FC (Dublin)

Quarter-Finals

Bray Wanderers AFC (Bray)	0-4	Bohemian FC (Dublin)
Derry City FC (Derry)	3-1	St. Patrick's Athletic FC (Dublin)
Finn Harps FC (Ballybofey)	1-1, 0-2	Cork City FC (Cork)
Kilkenny City FC (Kilkenny)	0-1	Shamrock Rovers FC (Dublin)

Round 3

Bohemian FC (Dublin)	2-0	University College Dublin AFC (Dublin)
Derry City FC (Derry)	3-0	Waterford United FC (Waterford)
Fairview Rangers FC (Limerick)	0-2	Finn Harps FC (Ballybofey)
Kilkenny City FC (Kilkenny)	1-0	Longford Town FC (Longford)
Monaghan United FC (Monaghan)	1-1, 0-3	Cork City FC (Cork)
St. Patrick's Athletic FC (Dublin)	2-1	Shelbourne FC (Dublin)
Shamrock Rovers FC (Dublin)	2-0	Cobh Ramblers FC (Cobh)
Sligo Rovers FC (Sligo)	0-2	Bray Wanderers AFC (Bray)

Round 2

Athlone Town AFC (Athlone)	0-0, 0-3 (aet)	Kilkenny City FC (Kilkenny)
Bohemian FC (Dublin)	6-0	Garda AFC (Dublin)
Bray Wanderers AFC (Bray)	2-0	Glebe North FC (Balbriggan)
C.I.E. Ranch (Dublin)	1-5	Longford Town FC (Longford)
Drogheda United FC (Drogheda)	1-3	Derry City FC (Derry)
Dundalk FC (Dundalk)	2-2, 1-2 (aet)	Shamrock Rovers FC (Dublin)
Fairview Rangers FC (Limerick)	4-1	Dublin City FC (Dublin)
Finn Harps FC (Ballybofey)	1-0	Leeds AFC (Cork)
Glenmore Dundrum FC (Dublin)	0-9	Cork City FC (Cork)
Greystones AFC (Greystones)	0-1	Sligo Rovers FC (Sligo)
Limerick FC (Limerick)	1-1, 2-2 (aet)	Waterford United FC (Waterford)
	(Waterford United won 4-2 on penalties)	
Malahide United FC (Malahide)	0-1	Cobh Ramblers FC (Cobh)
Monaghan United FC (Monaghan)	1-0	Midleton FC (Midleton)
St. Patrick's Athletic FC (Dublin)	2-2, 1-0 (aet)	Galway United FC (Galway)
Shelbourne FC (Dublin)	8-0	Rockmount FC (Whitechurch)
University College Dublin AFC (Dublin)	2-1	Kildare County FC (Newbridge)

Round 1

Ashtown Villa FC (Dublin)	1-2	Glebe North FC (Balbriggan)
Ballincollig FC (Cork)	1-2	Leeds AFC (Cork)
Cherry Orchard FC (Dublin)	0-3	C.I.E. Ranch (Dublin)
Douglas Hall FC (Cork)	2-4	Malahide United FC (Malahide)
Drogheda Town FC (Drogheda)	1-2	Midleton FC (Midleton)
Fairview Rangers FC (Limerick)	3-1	Peake Villa FC (Thurles)
Fanad United FC (Ballylar)	0-2	Greystones AFC (Greystones)
Garda AFC (Dublin)	4-1	Ballynanty Rovers FC (Limerick)
Rockmount FC (Whitechurch)	3-2	St. Michael's FC (Tipperary)
Workmans'/Dunleary (Dun Laoghaire)	1-2	Glenmore Dundrum FC (Dublin)

(all other clubs received byes)

2003

FAI Cup Final (Lansdowne Road, Dublin – 26/10/03 – 15,000)

LONGFORD TOWN FC (LONGFORD)	2-0	St. Patrick's Athletic FC (Dublin)

Francis 32', Barrett 90'

Longford Town: O'Brien, Murphy, Ferguson, McGovern, Dillon, Kirby (Lavine 83'), Perth, Keogh, Prunty, Barrett, Francis.

St. Patrick's Athletic: Adamson, Prenderville, Maguire, Foley, Delaney (Foy, 79), Dunne, Fahy, Byrne (Donnelly 31'), Osam, McPhee (Freeman 55'), Bird.

Semi-Finals

Bohemian FC (Dublin)	1-1, 3-4 (aet)	St. Patrick's Athletic FC (Dublin)
Longford Town FC (Longford)	1-0	Galway United FC (Galway)

Quarter-Finals

Drogheda United FC (Drogheda)	1-1, 0-3	Bohemian FC (Dublin)
Longford Town FC (Longford)	3-1	Waterford United FC (Waterford)
St. Patrick's Athletic FC (Dublin)	2-1	Kildare County FC (Newbridge)
Sligo Rovers FC (Sligo)	1-2	Galway United FC (Galway)

Round 3

Bohemian FC (Dublin)	3-0	Skerries Town FC (Skerries)
Bray Wanderers AFC (Bray)	1-2	Waterford United FC (Waterford)
Drogheda United FC (Drogheda)	2-0	University College Dublin AFC (Dublin)
Galway United FC (Galway)	2-1	Derry City FC (Derry)
Kildare County FC (Newbridge)	1-0	Cherry Orchard FC (Dublin)
Longford Town FC (Longford)	2-1	Limerick FC Limerick)
St. Patrick's Athletic FC (Dublin)	3-0	Dublin City FC (Dublin)
Sligo Rovers FC (Sligo)	0-0, 3-2 (aet)	Shelbourne FC (Dublin)

Round 2

Bray Wanderers AFC (Bray)	6-3	Athlone Town AFC (Athlone)
Cherry Orchard FC (Dublin)	3-0	St. Mochta's FC (Dublin)
Cork City FC (Cork)	0-2	Shelbourne FC (Dublin)
Derry City FC (Derry)	0-0, 1-0	Cobh Ramblers FC (Cobh)
Dundalk FC (Dundalk)	0-2	Bohemian FC (Dublin)
Everton AFC (Cork)	1-3	Waterford United FC (Waterford)
Finn Harps FC (Ballybofey)	1-2	Drogheda United FC (Drogheda)
Kildare County FC (Newbridge)	3-1	Crumlin United FC (Dublin)
Limerick FC (Limerick)	2-1	Kilkenny City FC (Kilkenny)
Loughshinney United FC (Dublin)	0-2	Galway United FC (Galway)
Moyle Park College AFC (Dublin)	0-2	Sligo Rovers FC (Sligo)
Portmarnock FC (Portmarnock)	0-1	Dublin City FC (Dublin)
St. Patrick's Athletic FC (Dublin)	3-2	Shamrock Rovers FC (Dublin)
Skerries Town FC (Skerries)	1-0	Monaghan United FC (Monaghan)
Tolka Rovers FC (Dublin)	1-4	Longford Town FC (Longford)
University College Dublin AFC (Dublin)	2-0	Belgrove AFC Dublin)

Round 1

Ballymun United FC (Dublin)	2-2, 2-3	Tolka Rovers FC (Dublin)
Clover United FC (Dublin)	0-1	Crumlin United FC (Dublin)
Loughshinney United FC (Dublin)	3-2	Fanad United FC (Ballylar)
Moyle Park College AFC (Dublin)	1-1, 4-2	Fairview Rangers FC (Limerick)
Newbridge Town FC (Newbridge)	0-3	Everton AFC (Cork)
Portmarnock FC (Portmarnock)	1-1, 3-1	Rockmount FC (Whitechurch)
Skerries Town FC (Skerries)	2-0	Glebe North FC (Balbriggan)
Southend United FC (Waterford)	1-1, 1-2	St. Mochta's FC (Dublin)
U.C.C.	1-1, 1-2	Cherry Orchard FC (Dublin)

(all other clubs received byes)

2004

FAI Cup Final (Lansdowne Road, Dublin – 24/10/2004 – 10,000)

LONGFORD TOWN FC (LONGFORD)	2-1	Waterford United FC (Waterford)
Kirby 86', Keegan 88'		*Bruton 62'*

Longford: O'Brien, Murphy, Prunty, Dillon, Gartland, Martin (Keegan 70), Kirby, Fitzgerald, Barrett (Perth 90+4), Lavine, Baker.

Waterford: Connor, Whelehan, Frost, Breen, Purcell, Reynolds, Carey (Sullivan 61), Mulcahy, Quitongo (Waters 61), Bruton, Murphy.

Semi-Finals

Derry City FC (Derry)	1-2	Waterford United FC (Waterford)
Longford Town FC (Longford)	0-0, 2-1	Drogheda United FC (Drogheda)

Quarter-Finals

Derry City FC (Derry)	1-0	Kildare County FC (Newbridge)
Longford Town FC (Longford)	2-2, 3-0	Athlone Town AFC (Athlone)
University College Dublin AFC (Dublin)	0-0, 2-3	Drogheda United FC (Drogheda)
Waterford United FC (Waterford)	2-2, 2-1	Rockmount FC (Whitechurch)

Round 3

Athlone Town AFC (Athlone)	1-0	Cobh Ramblers FC (Cobh)
Bohemian FC (Dublin)	0-1	Kildare County FC (Newbridge)
Drogheda United FC (Drogheda)	2-0	St. Patrick's Athletic FC (Dublin)
Longford Town FC (Longford)	1-1, 1-0	Shamrock Rovers FC (Dublin)
Rockmount FC (Whitechurch)	2-0	Monaghan United FC (Monaghan)
Shelbourne FC (Dublin)	1-1, 0-0 (aet)	Derry City FC (Derry)

(Derry City FC won 5-3 on penalties)

University College Dublin FC (Dublin)	5-0	Drumcondra AFC (Dublin)
Waterford United FC (Waterford)	7-2	Kilkenny City FC (Kilkenny)

Round 2

Athlone Town AFC (Athlone)	3-0	Tullamore FC (Tullamore)
Bohemian FC (Dublin)	8-0	Ringmahon Rangers FC (Whitechurch)
Bray Wanderers AFC (Bray)	0-2	Kilkenny City FC (Kilkenny)
Cobh Ramblers FC (Cobh)	3-3, 2-2 (aet)	Limerick FC (Limerick)
	(Cobh Ramblers FC won 3-2 on penalties)	
Dundalk FC (Dundalk)	0-0, 2-3	Drogheda United FC (Drogheda)
Galway United FC (Galway)	0-1	Derry City FC (Derry)
Kildare County FC (Newbridge)	4-0	Glebe North FC (Balbriggan)
Leeds AFC (Cork)	0-3	Longford Town FC (Longford)
Monaghan United FC (Monaghan)	1-0	Dublin City FC (Dublin)
Quay Celtic FC (Dundalk)	3-4	Drumcondra AFC (Dublin)
Rockmount FC (Whitechurch)	3-1	Portmarnock FC (Portmarnock)
St. Patrick's Athletic FC (Dublin)	4-1	Wayside Celtic FC (Dublin)
Shamrock Rovers FC (Dublin)	3-0	Carrick United FC (Carrick-on-Suir)
Shelbourne FC (Dublin)	4-1	Finn Harps FC (Ballybofey)
University College Dublin AFC (Dublin)	1-0	Cork City FC (Cork)
Waterford United FC (Waterford)	2-1	Sligo Rovers FC (Sligo)

Round 1

Belgrove AFC (Dublin)	0-1	Leeds AFC (Cork)
Carrick United FC (Carrick-on-Suir)	3-2	Bluebell United FC (Dublin)
Cherry Orchard FC (Dublin)	1-2	Glebe North FC (Balbriggan)
Drumcondra AFC (Dublin)	1-1, 2-0	Letterkenny Rovers FC (Letterkenny)
Fairview Rangers FC (Limerick)	0-2	Wayside Celtic FC (Dublin)
Freebooters FC (Kilkenny)	3-3, w/o	Portmarnock FC (Portmarnock)
Moyle Park College AFC (Dublin)	1-1, 1-2	Quay Celtic FC (Dundalk)
Ringmahon Rangers FC (Whitechurch)	3-0	C.Y.M Terenure FC (Dublin)
Rockmount FC (Whitechurch)	2-2, 3-2	College Corinthians AFC (Cork)
Tullamore FC (Tullamore)	1-1, 1-0	Bangor Celtic FC (Dublin)
(all other clubs received byes)		

Republic of Ireland International Line-ups 2000-2005

23rd February 2000
v CZECH REPUBLIC *Dublin*

A. Kelly	Blackburn Rovers
K. Cunningham	Wimbledon
G. Kelly	Leeds United
I. Harte	Leeds United
P. Butler (sub. P. Babb)	Sunderland
M. Kennedy (sub. J. McAteer)	Manchester City
Roy Keane	Manchester United
M. Kinsella	Charlton Athletic
K. Kilbane (sub. S. Staunton)	Sunderland
N. Quinn	Sunderland
Robbie Keane (sub. D. Connolly)	Coventry City

Result 3-2   Rada (og), Harte, Robbie Keane

26th April 2000
v GREECE *Dublin*

S. Given (sub. D. Kiely)	Newcastle United
K. Cunningham	Wimbledon
G. Breen	Coventry City
S. Staunton	Liverpool
R. Dunne	Everton
M. Kinsella	Charlton Athletic
K. Kilbane	Sunderland
B. Quinn (sub. R. Delap)	Coventry City
S. Finnan (sub. G. Doherty)	Fulham
Robbie Keane	Coventry City
D. Connolly (sub. A. Mahon)	Excelsior

Result 0-1

30th May 2000
v SCOTLAND *Dublin*

A. Kelly	Blackburn Rovers
G. Breen (sub. R. Dunne)	Coventry City
K. Kilbane	Sunderland
S. Carr	Tottenham Hotspur
P. Babb	Liverpool
M. Kennedy (sub. D. Duff)	Manchester City
J. McAteer	Blackburn Rovers
S. Finnan	Fulham
S. McPhail (sub. T. Phelan)	Leeds United
N. Quinn (sub. D. Foley)	Sunderland
Robbie Keane	Coventry City

Result 1-2   Kennedy

4th June 2000
v MEXICO *Chicago*

D. Kiely	Charlton Athletic
G. Breen	Coventry City
S. Carr	Tottenham Hotspur
R. Dunne (sub. P. Babb)	Everton
T. Phelan	Fulham
M. Kennedy	Manchester City
M. Holland	Ipswich Town
J. McAteer	Blackburn Rovers
B. Quinn (sub. K. Kilbane)	Coventry City
N. Quinn	Sunderland
Robbie Keane (sub. D. Foley)	Coventry City

Result 2-2   Dunne, Foley

6th June 2000
v U.S.A. *Foxboro*

A. Kelly	Blackburn Rovers
G. Breen	Coventry City
S. Carr	Tottenham Hotspur
P. Babb	Liverpool
T. Phelan	Fulham
K. Kilbane	Sunderland
M. Holland	Ipswich Town
S. McPhail (sub. J. McAteer)	Leeds United
G. Farrelly (sub. M. Kennedy)	Bolton Wanderers
G. Doherty (sub. N. Quinn)	Tottenham Hotspur
D. Foley (sub. B. Quinn)	Watford

Result 1-1   Foley

11th June 2000
v SOUTH AFRICA *New Jersey*

S. Given	Newcastle United
G. Breen	Coventry City
S. Carr	Tottenham Hotspur
P. Babb	Liverpool
T. Phelan	Fulham
M. Holland	Ipswich Town
J. McAteer (sub. M. Kennedy)	Blackburn Rovers
A. Mahon (sub. K. Kilbane)	Tranmere Rovers
S. McPhail (sub. B. Quinn)	Leeds United
N. Quinn (sub. G. Doherty)	Sunderland
D. Foley (sub. Robbie Keane)	Watford

Result 2-1   McPhail, N. Quinn

2nd September 2000
v HOLLAND (WCQ) *Amsterdam*

A. Kelly	Blackburn Rovers
S. Carr	Tottenham Hotspur
G. Breen	Coventry City
R. Dunne	Everton
I. Harte	Leeds United
J. McAteer (sub. G. Kelly)	Blackburn Rovers
Roy Keane	Manchester United
M. Kinsella	Charlton Athletic
K. Kilbane (sub. S. Staunton)	Sunderland
N. Quinn (sub. D. Connolly)	Sunderland
Robbie Keane	Internazionale

Result 2-2   Robbie Keane, McAteer

7th October 2000
v PORTUGAL (WCQ) *Lisbon*

A. Kelly	Blackburn Rovers
S. Carr	Tottenham Hotspur
G. Breen	Coventry City
R. Dunne	Everton
I. Harte	Leeds United
J. McAteer (sub. D. Duff)	Blackburn Rovers
Roy Keane	Manchester United
M. Kinsella	Charlton Athletic
K. Kilbane	Sunderland
N. Quinn (sub. M. Holland)	Sunderland
Robbie Keane (sub. S. Finnan)	Internazionale

Result 1-1   Holland

11th October 2000
v ESTONIA (WCQ) *Dublin*

A. Kelly	Blackburn Rovers
S. Carr	Tottenham Hotspur
G. Breen	Coventry City
R. Dunne	Everton
I. Harte	Leeds United
J. McAteer (sub. D. Duff)	Blackburn Rovers
Roy Keane	Manchester United
M. Kinsella	Charlton Athletic
K. Kilbane (sub. S. Finnan)	Sunderland
N. Quinn	Sunderland
Robbie Keane (sub. D. Foley)	Internazionale

Result 2-0   Kinsella, Dunne

15th November 2000
v FINLAND *Dublin*

S. Given	Newcastle United
G. Breen	Coventry City
R. Dunne	Manchester City
I. Harte (sub. S. Staunton)	Leeds United
G. Kelly (sub. J. McAteer)	Leeds United
M. Kinsella	Charlton Athletic
K. Kilbane	Sunderland
M. Holland	Ipswich Town
S. Finnan	Fulham
Robbie Keane (sub. D. Connolly)	Internazionale
D. Foley (sub. L. Carsley)	Blackburn Rovers

Result 3-0   Finnan, Kilbane, Staunton

24th March 2001
v CYPRUS (WCQ) *Nicosia*

S. Given	Newcastle United
G. Breen	Coventry City
I. Harte	Leeds United
G. Kelly	Leeds United
K. Cunningham	Wimbledon
J. McAteer (sub. M. Holland)	Blackburn Rovers
Roy Keane	Manchester United
M. Kinsella	Charlton Athletic
K. Kilbane (sub. D. Duff)	Sunderland
Robbie Keane (sub. G. Doherty)	Leeds United
D. Connolly	Feyenoord

Result 4-0   Roy Keane 2, Harte (pen), Kelly

28th March 2001
v ANDORRA (WCQ) *Barcelona*

S. Given	Newcastle United
G. Breen	Coventry City
I. Harte	Leeds United
G. Kelly	Leeds United
K. Cunningham	Wimbledon
Roy Keane	Manchester United
K. Kilbane (sub. S. Finnan)	Sunderland
M. Holland	Ipswich Town
D. Duff	Blackburn Rovers
Robbie Keane	Leeds United
D. Connolly (sub. G. Doherty)	Feyenoord

Result 3-0   Harte (pen), Kilbane, Holland

25th April 2001
v ANDORRA (WCQ) *Dublin*

S. Given	Newcastle United
G. Breen (sub. S. Staunton)	Coventry City
R. Dunne	Manchester City
I. Harte	Leeds United
G. Kelly	Leeds United
M. Kinsella (sub. S. Finnan)	Charlton Athletic
K. Kilbane	Sunderland
M. Holland	Ipswich Town
M. Kennedy (sub. S. Carr)	Manchester City
D. Connolly	Feyenoord
G. Doherty	Tottenham Hotspur

Result 3-1 Kilbane, Kinsella, Breen

2nd June 2001
v PORTUGAL (WCQ) *Dublin*

S. Given	Newcastle United
S. Carr	Tottenham Hotspur
R. Dunne	Manchester City
I. Harte	Leeds United
S. Staunton	Aston Villa
Roy Keane	Manchester United
M. Kinsella (sub. G. Doherty)	Charlton Athletic
K. Kilbane	Sunderland
G. Kelly	Leeds United
N. Quinn (sub. M. Holland)	Sunderland
Robbie Keane (sub. D. Duff)	Leeds United

Result 1-1 Roy Keane

6th June 2001
v ESTONIA (WCQ) *Tallinn*

S. Given	Newcastle United
S. Carr	Tottenham Hotspur
R. Dunne	Manchester City
I. Harte	Leeds United
S. Staunton	Aston Villa
M. Kinsella	Charlton Athletic
K. Kilbane	Sunderland
G. Kelly	Leeds United
M. Holland	Ipswich Town
N. Quinn (sub. G. Doherty)	Sunderland
D. Duff (sub. A. O'Brien)	Blackburn Rovers

Result 2-0 Dunne, Holland

15th August 2001
v CROATIA *Dublin*

S. Given (sub. A. Kelly)	Newcastle United
G. Kelly (sub. J. O'Shea)	Leeds United
I. Harte (sub. S. McPhail)	Leeds United
R. Dunne (sub. A. O'Brien)	Manchester City
S. Staunton	Aston Villa
Roy Keane (sub. J. McAteer)	Manchester United
S. Reid (sub. S. Finnan)	Millwall
M. Kennedy (sub. K. Kilbane)	Wolverhampton Wands.
L. Carsley	Coventry City
D. Duff (sub. D. Connolly)	Blackburn Rovers
Robbie Keane (sub. C. Morrison)	Leeds United

Result 2-2 Duff, Morrison

1st September 2001
v HOLLAND (WCQ) *Dublin*

S. Given	Newcastle United
G. Kelly	Leeds United
I. Harte (sub. N. Quinn)	Leeds United
R. Dunne	Manchester City
S. Staunton	Aston Villa
Roy Keane	Manchester United
J. McAteer (sub. A. O'Brien)	Blackburn Rovers
K. Kilbane	Sunderland
M. Holland	Ipswich Town
D. Duff	Blackburn Rovers
Robbie Keane (sub. S. Finnan)	Leeds United

Result 1-0 McAteer

6th October 2001
v CYPRUS (WCQ) *Dublin*

S. Given	Newcastle United
I. Harte	Leeds United
S. Staunton	Aston Villa
S. Finnan	Fulham
G. Breen	Coventry City
Roy Keane	Manchester United
M. Kennedy (sub. L. Carsley)	Wolverhampton Wands.
K. Kilbane (sub. S. McPhail)	Sunderland
M. Holland	Ipswich Town
D. Connolly	Wimbledon
N. Quinn (sub. C. Morrison)	Sunderland

Result 4-0 Harte, Quinn, Connolly, Keane

10th November 2001
v IRAN (WCQ) *Dublin*

S. Given	Newcastle United
I. Harte	Leeds United
S. Staunton (sub. K. Cunningham)	Aston Villa
S. Finnan	Fulham
G. Breen	Coventry City
Roy Keane	Manchester United
J. McAteer (sub. G. Kelly)	Sunderland
K. Kilbane	Sunderland
M. Holland	Ipswich Town
Robbie Keane	Leeds United
N. Quinn	Sunderland

Result 2-0   Harte (pen), Robbie Keane

15th November 2001
v IRAN (WCQ) *Tehran*

S. Given	Newcastle United
I. Harte	Leeds United
S. Staunton	Aston Villa
S. Finnan	Fulham
G. Breen	Coventry City
J. McAteer	Sunderland
K. Kilbane (sub. G. Kelly)	Sunderland
M. Holland	Ipswich Town
M. Kinsella	Charlton Athletic
Robbie Keane (sub. C. Morrison)	Leeds United
D. Connolly	Wimbledon

Result 0-1

13th February 2002
v RUSSIA *Dublin*

S. Given (sub. D. Kiely)	Newcastle United
I. Harte (sub. J. McAteer (sub. N. Quinn))	Leeds United
S. Finnan (sub. S. Staunton)	Fulham
A. O'Brien (sub. R. Dunne)	Newcastle United
K. Cunningham (sub. G. Breen)	Wimbledon
Roy Keane (sub. M. Holland)	Manchester United
S. Reid	Millwall
K. Kilbane (sub. M. Kennedy)	Sunderland
C. Healy (sub. L. Carsley)	Celtic
D. Duff (sub. C. Morrison)	Blackburn Rovers
Robbie Keane (sub. R. Sadlier)	Leeds United

Result 2-0   Reid, Robbie Keane

27th March 2002
v DENMARK *Dublin*

D. Kiely (sub. N. Colgan)	Charlton Athletic
G. Kelly	Leeds United
I. Harte	Leeds United
S. Staunton	Aston Villa
K. Cunningham	Wimbledon
D. Duff (sub. R. Dunne)	Blackburn Rovers
J. McAteer (sub. S. Reid)	Sunderland
M. Holland	Ipswich Town
M. Kinsella (sub. C. Healy)	Charlton Athletic
Robbie Keane (sub. D. Connolly)	Leeds United
C. Morrison	Crystal Palace

Result 3-0   Harte, Robbie Keane, Morrison

17th April 2002
v U.S.A. *Dublin*

S. Given	Newcastle United
I. Harte (sub. S. Staunton)	Leeds United
S. Finnan (sub. G. Kelly)	Fulham
A. O'Brien (sub. K. Cunningham)	Newcastle United
G. Breen (sub. G. Doherty)	Coventry City
K. Kilbane (sub. S. Reid)	Sunderland
M. Kinsella (sub. M. Holland)	Charlton Athletic
C. Healy	Celtic
R. Delap	Southampton
D. Duff (sub. D. Connolly)	Blackburn Rovers
Robbie Keane (sub. C. Morrison)	Leeds United

Result 2-1   Kinsella, Doherty

16th May 2002
v NIGERIA *Dublin*

S. Given	Newcastle United
I. Harte	Leeds United
S. Staunton	Aston Villa
S. Finnan	Fulham
K. Cunningham	Wimbledon
Roy Keane (sub. M. Kinsella)	Manchester United
J. McAteer (sub. S. Reid)	Sunderland
K. Kilbane (sub. G. Kelly)	Sunderland
M. Holland	Ipswich Town
D. Duff (sub. D. Connolly)	Blackburn Rovers
Robbie Keane (sub. C. Morrison)	Leeds United

Result 1-2   Reid

1st June 2002
v CAMEROON (WC) *Niigata*

S. Given	Newcastle United
G. Kelly	Leeds United
I. Harte (sub. S. Reid)	Leeds United
S. Staunton	Aston Villa
G. Breen	Coventry City
J. McAteer (sub. S. Finnan)	Sunderland
K. Kilbane	Sunderland
M. Holland	Ipswich Town
M. Kinsella	Charlton Athletic
D. Duff	Blackburn Rovers
Robbie Keane	Leeds United

Result 1-1   Holland

5th June 2002
v GERMANY (WC) *Ibaraki*

S. Given	Newcastle United
I. Harte (sub. S. Reid)	Leeds United
S. Staunton (sub. K. Cunningham)	Aston Villa
S. Finnan	Fulham
G. Breen	Coventry City
G. Kelly (sub. N. Quinn)	Leeds United
K. Kilbane	Sunderland
M. Holland	Ipswich Town
M. Kinsella	Charlton Athletic
D. Duff	Blackburn Rovers
Robbie Keane	Leeds United

Result 1-1   Robbie Keane

11th June 2002
v SAUDI ARABIA (WC) *Yokohama*

S. Given	Newcastle United
I. Harte (sub. N. Quinn)	Leeds United
S. Staunton	Aston Villa
S. Finnan	Fulham
G. Breen	Coventry City
G. Kelly (sub. J. McAteer)	Leeds United
K. Kilbane	Sunderland
M. Holland	Ipswich Town
M. Kinsella (sub. L. Carsley)	Charlton Athletic
D. Duff	Blackburn Rovers
Robbie Keane	Leeds United

Result 3-0   Robbie Keane, Breen, Duff

16th June 2002
v SPAIN (WC) *Suwon*

S. Given	Newcastle United
I. Harte (sub. D. Connolly)	Leeds United
S. Staunton (sub. K. Cunningham)	Aston Villa
S. Finnan	Fulham
G. Breen	Coventry City
G. Kelly (sub. N. Quinn)	Leeds United
K. Kilbane	Sunderland
M. Holland	Ipswich Town
M. Kinsella	Charlton Athletic
D. Duff	Blackburn Rovers
Robbie Keane	Leeds United

Result 1-1 (aet)   Robbie Keane
Spain won 3-2 on penalties

21st August 2002
v FINLAND *Helsinki*

D. Kiely (sub. S. Given)	Charlton Athletic
G. Kelly	Leeds United
K. Cunningham (sub. G. Doherty)	Birmingham City
G. Breen	West Ham United
I. Harte (sub. G. Barrett)	Leeds United
J. McAteer (R. Delap)	Sunderland
M. Kinsella (sub. S. McPhail)	Charlton Athletic
L. Carsley (sub. M. Holland)	Everton
T. Butler (sub. K. Kilbane)	Sunderland
Robbie Keane (sub. J. Goodwin)	Leeds United
D. Duff (sub. C. Healy)	Blackburn Rovers

Result 3-0   Keane, Healy, Barrett

7th September 2002
v RUSSIA (ECQ) *Moscow*

S. Given	Newcastle United
K. Cunningham	Birmingham City
G. Breen	West Ham United
I. Harte	Leeds United
S. Finnan	Fulham
J. McAteer (sub. G. Doherty)	Sunderland
M. Kinsella	Aston Villa
K. Kilbane (sub. P. Babb)	Sunderland
M. Holland	Ipswich Town
Robbie Keane	Tottenham Hotspur
D. Duff (sub. C. Morrison)	Blackburn Rovers

Result 2-4   Doherty, Morrison

16th October 2002
v SWITZERLAND (ECQ) *Dublin*

S. Given	Newcastle United
G. Kelly	Leeds United
K. Cunningham	Birmingham City
G. Breen	West Ham United
I. Harte (sub. G. Doherty)	Leeds United
M. Kinsella	Aston Villa
C. Healy	Celtic
K. Kilbane (sub. C. Morrison)	Sunderland
M. Holland	Ipswich Town
Robbie Keane	Tottenham Hotspur
D. Duff (sub. T. Butler)	Blackburn Rovers

Result 1-2   Magnin (og)

20th November 2002
v GREECE *Athens*

S. Given	Newcastle United
K. Cunningham	Birmingham City
S. Finnan	Fulham
R. Dunne	Manchester City
J. O'Shea	Manchester United
L. Carsley	Everton
C. Healy	Celtic
S. McPhail	Leeds United
M. Holland	Ipswich Town
G. Doherty	Tottenham Hotspur
G. Crowe (sub. R. Delap)	Bohemians

Result 0-0

12th February 2003
v SCOTLAND *Glasgow*

D. Kiely (sub. N. Colgan)	Charlton Athletic
S. Carr	Tottenham Hotspur
J. O'Shea (sub. R. Dunne)	Manchester United
G. Breen (sub. A. O'Brien)	West Ham United
I. Harte	Leeds United
S. Reid (sub. L. Carsley)	Millwall
M. Holland	Ipswich Town
M. Kinsella (sub. C. Healy)	Aston Villa
K. Kilbane	Sunderland
G. Doherty (sub. D. Connolly)	Tottenham Hotspur
C. Morrison	Birmingham City

Result 2-0   Kilbane, Morrison

29th March 2003
v GEORGIA (ECQ) *Tbilisi*

S. Given	Newcastle United
S. Carr	Tottenham Hotspur
K. Cunningham	Birmingham City
G. Breen	West Ham United
J. O'Shea	Manchester United
L. Carsley	Everton
M. Holland	Ipswich Town
M. Kinsella	Aston Villa
K. Kilbane	Sunderland
G. Doherty	Tottenham Hotspur
D. Duff	Blackburn Rovers

Result 2-1   Duff, Doherty

2nd April 2003
v ALBANIA (ECQ) *Tirana*

S. Given	Newcastle United
S. Carr	Tottenham Hotspur
K. Cunningham	Birmingham City
G. Breen	West Ham United
J. O'Shea	Manchester United
L. Carsley	Everton
M. Holland	Ipswich Town
M. Kinsella	Aston Villa
K. Kilbane	Sunderland
Robbie Keane (sub. G. Doherty)	Tottenham Hotspur
D. Duff	Blackburn Rovers

Result 0-0

30th April 2003
v NORWAY *Dublin*

S. Given (sub. N. Colgan)	Newcastle United
S. Carr	
G. Breen	
R. Dunne	
I. Harte (sub. S. Finnan)	Leeds United
M. Holland	
M. Kinsella (sub. L. Carsley)	Aston Villa
K. Kilbane (sub. A. Quinn)	Sunderland
D. Duff (sub. C. Healy)	Blackburn Rovers
D. Connolly (sub. A. Lee)	Wimbledon
Robbie Keane (sub. G. Crowe)	Tottenham Hotspur

Result 1-0   Duff

7th June 2003
v ALBANIA (ECQ) *Dublin*

S. Given	Newcastle United
S. Carr	Tottenham Hotspur
G. Breen	West Ham United
K. Cunningham	Birmingham City
J. O'Shea	Manchester United
M. Holland	Ipswich Town
M. Kinsella (sub. L. Carsley)	Aston Villa
K. Kilbane (sub. S. Reid)	Sunderland
D. Duff	Blackburn Rovers
D. Connolly (sub. G. Doherty)	Wimbledon
Robbie Keane	Tottenham Hotspur

Result 2-1   Keane, Aliaj (og)

11th June 2003
v GEORGIA (ECQ) *Dublin*

S. Given	Newcastle United
S. Carr	Tottenham Hotspur
G. Breen	West Ham United
K. Cunningham	Birmingham City
J. O'Shea	Manchester United
L. Carsley	Everton
C. Healy (sub. M. Kinsella)	Celtic
M. Holland	Ipswich Town
K. Kilbane	Sunderland
G. Doherty (sub. A. Lee)	Tottenham Hotspur
Robbie Keane	Tottenham Hotspur

Result 2-0   Doherty, Keane

19th August 2003
v AUSTRALIA *Dublin*

N. Colgan	Stockport County
S. Carr (sub. I. Harte)	Tottenham Hotspur
G. Breen (sub. A. O'Brien)	Sunderland
K. Cunningham (sub. R. Dunne)	Birmingham City
J. O'Shea	Manchester United
S. Finnan (sub. K. Kilbane)	Fulham
M. Kinsella	Aston Villa
M. Holland (sub. C. Healy)	Charlton Athletic
D. Duff (sub. A. Quinn)	Chelsea
Robbie Keane (sub. D. Connolly)	Tottenham Hotspur
G. Doherty (sub. C. Morrison)	Tottenham Hotspur

Result 2-1   O'Shea, Morrison

6th September 2003
v RUSSIA (ECQ) *Dublin*

S. Given	Newcastle United
S. Carr	Tottenham Hotspur
G. Breen	Sunderland
K. Cunningham	Birmingham City
J. O'Shea (sub. I. Harte)	Manchester United
L. Carsley (sub. S. Reid)	Everton
C. Healy	Sunderland
M. Holland	Charlton Athletic
K. Kilbane	Everton
D. Duff	Chelsea
C. Morrison (sub. G. Doherty)	Birmingham City

Result 1-1   Duff

9th September 2003
v TURKEY *Dublin*

N. Colgan (sub. J. Murphy)	Stockport County
S. Finnan	Fulham
G. Breen (sub. C. Morrison)	Sunderland
A. O'Brien (sub. R. Dunne)	Newcastle United
I. Harte (sub. S. Carr)	Leeds United
D. Duff (sub. S. Reid)	Chelsea
C. Healy (sub. S. McPhail)	Sunderland
M. Kinsella	Aston Villa
K. Kilbane	Everton
D. Connolly	West Ham United
G. Doherty	Tottenham Hotspur

Result 2-2   Connolly, Dunne

11th October 2003
v SWITZERLAND (ECQ) *Basel*

S. Given	Newcastle United
S. Carr	Tottenham Hotspur
G. Breen	Sunderland
J. O'Shea	Manchester United
I. Harte	Leeds United
D. Duff	Chelsea
M. Holland (sub. M. Kinsella)	Charlton Athletic
C. Healy	Sunderland
K. Kilbane (sub. S. Finnan)	Everton
D. Connolly (sub. C. Morrison)	West Ham United
Robbie Keane	Tottenham Hotspur

Result 0-2

18th November 2003
v CANADA *Dublin*

S. Given (sub. N. Colgan)	Newcastle United
S. Carr (sub. I. Harte)	Tottenham Hotspur
K. Cunningham	Birmingham City
R. Dunne	Manchester City
J. O'Shea (sub. J. Thompson)	Manchester United
S. Reid (sub. R. Delap)	Blackburn Rovers
G. Kavanagh (sub. M. Holland)	Cardiff City
A. Reid (sub. S. McPhail)	Nottingham Forest
D. Duff (sub. K. Kilbane)	Chelsea
Robbie Keane	Tottenham Hotspur
G. Doherty (sub. C. Morrison)	Tottenham Hotspur

Result 3-0   Duff, Keane 2

18th February 2004
v BRAZIL *Dublin*

S. Given	Newcastle United
S. Carr	Tottenham Hotspur
K. Cunningham	Birmingham City
A. O'Brien	Newcastle United
J. O'Shea	Manchester United
M. Holland	Charlton Athletic
G. Kavanagh	Cardiff City
K. Kilbane	Everton
A. Reid (sub. J. McAteer)	Nottingham Forest
C. Morrison	Birmingham City
Robbie Keane	Tottenham Hotspur

Result 0-0

31st March 2004
v CZECH REPUBLIC *Dublin*

S. Given (sub. P. Kenny)	Newcastle United
A. Maybury	Heart of Midlothian
G. Doherty (sub. L. Miller)	Tottenham Hotspur
K. Cunningham	Birmingham City
I. Harte	Leeds United
A. Reid (sub. R. Delap)	Nottingham Forest
M. Holland	Charlton Athletic
K. Kilbane	Everton
D. Duff (sub. M. Kinsella)	Chelsea
C. Morrison (sub. A. Lee)	Birmingham City
Robbie Keane	Tottenham Hotspur

Result 2-1   Harte, Keane

30th April 2004
v POLAND *Bydgoszcz*

S. Given (sub. N. Colgan)	Newcastle United
J. O'Shea	Manchester United
K. Cunningham	Birmingham City
G. Doherty (sub. A. O'Brien)	Tottenham Hotspur
I. Harte (sub. A. Maybury)	Leeds United
S. Reid	Blackburn Rovers
M. Kinsella	West Bromwich Albion
L. Miller	Celtic
A. Reid (sub. J. Douglas)	Nottingham Forest
C. Morrison (sub. J. Byrne)	Birmingham City
A. Lee (sub. G. Barrett)	Cardiff City

Result 0-0

27th May 2004
v ROMANIA *Dublin*

S. Given	Newcastle United
S. Finnan	Fulham
A. O'Brien	Newcastle United
K. Cunningham	Birmingham City
A. Maybury	Heart of Midlothian
L. Miller	Celtic
Roy Keane	Manchester United
M. Holland	Charlton Athletic
A. Reid (sub. M. Rowlands)	Nottingham Forest
C. Morrison	Birmingham City
Robbie Keane	Tottenham Hotspur

Result 1-0   Holland

29th May 2004
v NIGERIA *London*

N. Colgan	Stockport County
S. Finnan	Fulham
K. Cunningham	Birmingham City
G. Doherty	Tottenham Hotspur
A. Maybury (sub. C. Clarke)	Heart of Midlothian
L. Miller (sub. M. Rowlands)	Celtic
M. Kinsella	West Bromwich Albion
M. Holland (sub. J. Douglas)	Charlton Athletic
S. McPhail	Leeds United
Robbie Keane (sub. G. Barrett)	Tottenham Hotspur
A. Lee	Cardiff City

Result 0-3

2nd June 2004
v JAMAICA _London_

P. Kenny	Sheffield United
A. Maybury	Heart of Midlothain
G. Doherty	Tottenham Hotspur
A. O'Brien	Newcastle United
J. O'Shea (sub. C. Clarke)	Manchester United
G. Barrett	Coventry City
M. Kinsella	West Bromwich Albion
A. Quinn (sub. M. Holland)	Sheffield Wednesday
A. Reid (sub. M. Rowlands)	Nottingham Forest
C. Morrison	Birmingham City
A. Lee (sub. A. McGeady)	Cardiff City

Result 1-0   Barrett

5th June 2004
v HOLLAND _Amsterdam_

S. Given	Newcastle United
S. Finnan	Fulham
A. O'Brien	Newcastle United
K. Cunningham	Birmingham City
A. Maybury	Heart of Midlothian
G. Barrett	Coventry City
M. Holland	Charlton Athletic
A. Quinn	Sheffield Wednesday
A. Reid (sub. M. Doyle)	Nottingham Forest
C. Morrision (sub. A. Lee)	Birmingham City
Robbie Keane	Tottenham Hotspur

Result 1-0   Keane

18th August 2004
v BULGARIA _Dublin_

S. Given (sub. P. Kenny)	Newcastle United
S. Finnan (sub. A. Quinn)	Fulham
G. Doherty (sub. G. Breen)	Tottenham Hotspur
K. Cunningham	Birmingham City
J. O'Shea	Manchester United
L. Miller (sub. S. Carr)	Manchester United
Roy Keane (G. Kavanagh)	Manchester United
K. Kilbane	Everton
A. Reid	Nottingham Forest
C. Morrison (sub. J. Macken)	Birmingham City
D. Duff	Chelsea

Result 1-1   Reid

4th September 2004
v CYPRUS (WCQ) _Dublin_

S. Given	Newcastle United
S. Carr (sub. S. Finnan)	Newcastle United
A. O'Brien	Newcastle United
K. Cunningham	Birmingham City
J. O'Shea (sub. A. Maybury)	Manchester United
A. Reid	Nottingham Forest
G. Kavanagh	Cardiff City
K. Kilbane	Everton
D. Duff	Chelsea
Robbie Keane	Tottenham Hotspur
C. Morrison (sub. A. Lee)	Birmingham City

Result 3-0   Morrison, Reid, Keane (pen)

8th September 2004
v SWITZERLAND (WCQ) _Basel_

S. Given	Newcastle United
S. Carr	Newcastle United
A. O'Brien	Newcastle United
K. Cunningham	Birmingham City
S. Finnan	Fulham
A. Reid (sub. G. Kavanagh	Nottingham Forest
Roy Keane	Manchester United
K. Kilbane	Everton
D. Duff	Chelsea
Robbie Keane	Tottenham Hotspur
C. Morrison (sub. G. Doherty)	Birmingham City

Result 1-1   Morrison

9th October 2004
v FRANCE (WCQ) _Paris_

S. Given	Newcastle United
S. Carr	Newcastle United
A. O'Brien	Newcaslte United
K. Cunningham	Birmingham City
J. O'Shea	Manchester United
S. Finnan	Fulham
Roy Keane	Manchester United
K. Kilbane	Everton
D. Duff	Chelsea
Robbie Keane	Tottenham Hotspur
C. Morrison (sub. A. Reid)	Birmingham City

Result 0-0

13th October 2004
v FAROE ISLANDS (WCQ) *Dublin*

S. Given	Newcastle United
S. Carr	Newcastle United
A. O'Brien	Newcastle United
K. Cunningham	Birmingham City
J. O'Shea (sub. L. Miller)	Manchester United
S. Finnan	Fulham
Roy Keane	Manchester United
K. Kilbane	Everton
D. Duff	Chelsea
Robbie Keane	Tottenham Hotspur
A. Reid (sub. G. Doherty)	Nottingham Forest

Result 2-0   Robbie Keane 2

16th November 2004
v CROATIA *Dublin*

P. Kenny (sub. S. Given)	Sheffield United
S. Finnan	Fulham
G. Breen (sub. K. Cunningham)	Sunderland
R. Dunne	Manchester United
J. O'Shea	Manchester United
L. Miller	Manchester United
G. Kavanagh	Cardiff City
K. Kilbane (sub. A. Quinn)	Everton
S. Elliott (sub. G. Barrett)	Sunderland
Robbie Keane (sub. A. McGeady)	Tottenham Hotspur
D. Duff	Chelsea

Result 1-0   Robbie Keane

9th February 2005
v PORTUGAL *Dublin*

S. Given	Newcastle United
S. Finnan	Fulham
K. Cunningham (sub. R. Dunne)	Birmingham City
A. O'Brien	Newcastle United
J. O'Shea	Manchester United
A. Reid	Tottenham Hotspur
M. Holland	Charlton Athletic
K. Kilbane (sub. G. Kavanagh)	Everton
D. Duff (sub. L. Miller)	Chelsea
Robbie Keane (sub. A. McGeady)	Tottenham Hotspur
C. Morrison	

Result 1-0   O'Brien

REPUBLIC OF IRELAND INTERNATIONAL FIXTURES

March 25th 2005

Israel vs Republic of Ireland U21   European U21 Championship Qualifier   Away

March 26th 2005

Israel vs Republic of Ireland   World Cup Qualifier   Away

March 29th 2005

Republic of Ireland vs China   Friendly   Lansdowne Road (Kick off 7:30pm)

May 29th 2005

Celtic XI vs Republic of Ireland XI   Jackie McNamara Testimonial   Glasgow (Scotland)

June 3rd 2005

Republic of Ireland U21 vs Israel   European U21 Championship Qualifier   Home

June 4th 2005

Republic of Ireland vs Israel   World Cup Qualifier   Lansdowne Road

June 8th 2005

Faroe Islands vs Republic of Ireland   World Cup Qualifier   Away

August 17th 2005

Republic of Ireland vs Italy   Friendly   Lansdowne Road (Kick off 7:30pm)

September 6th 2005

Republic of Ireland U21 vs France   European U21 Championship Qualifier   Home

September 7th 2005

Republic of Ireland vs France   World Cup Qualifier   Lansdowne Road

October 7th 2005

Cyprus vs Republic of Ireland U21   European U21 Championship Qualifier   Away

October 8th 2005

Cyprus vs Republic of Ireland   World Cup Qualifier   Away

October 11th 2005

Republic of Ireland U21 vs Switzerland   European U21 Championship Qualifier Home

October 12th 2005

Republic of Ireland vs Switzerland   World Cup Qualifier   Lansdowne Road

Premier Division Top-scorers 1995-96

1)	Stephen GEOGHEGAN	(Shelbourne FC)	20
2)	Mick O'BYRNE	(University College Dublin AFC)	16
3)	Padraig MORAN	(Sligo Rovers FC)	14
	Ricky O'FLAHERTY	(St. Patrick's Athletic FC)	14
5)	Tommy GAYNOR	(Athlone Town AFC)	12
	Ian GILZEAN	(Sligo Rovers FC)	12

Premier Division Top-scorers 1996-1997

1)	Stephen GEOGHEGAN	(Shelbourne FC)	16
2)	Tony COUSINS	(Shamrock Rovers FC)	15
	Peter HUTTON	(Derry City FC)	15
	Pat MORLEY	(Shelbourne FC)	15
	Martin REILLY	(St. Patrick's Athletic FC)	15

Premier Division Top-scorers 1997-1998

1)	Stephen GEOGHEGAN	(Shelbourne FC)	17
2)	Tony COUSINS	(Shamrock Rovers FC)	15
3)	Graham LAWLOR	(Bohemian FC)	13
4)	Ian GILZEAN	(St. Patrick's Athletic FC)	12
	Jason SHERLOCK	(University College Dublin AFC)	12

Premier Division Top-scorers 1998-1999

1)	Trevor MOLLOY	(St. Patrick's Athletic FC)	15
2)	Ian GILZEAN	(St. Patrick's Athletic FC)	12
3)	Kevin FLANAGAN	(Cork City FC)	11
	Marcus HALLOWS	(Sligo Rovers FC)	11
	Derek SWANS	(Bohemian FC)	11

Premier Division Top-scorers 1999-2000

1)	Pat MORLEY	(Cork City FC)	20
2)	Stephen GEOGHEGAN	(Shelbourne FC)	12
	James MULLIGAN	(Finn Harps FC)	12
4)	Padraig MORAN	(Sligo Rovers FC)	11
5)	Glen CROWE	(Bohemian FC)	9

Premier Division Top-scorers 2000-2001

1)	Glen CROWE	(Bohemian FC)	25
2)	Sean FRANCIS	(Shamrock Rovers FC)	13
	Liam KELLY	(St. Patrick's Athletic FC)	13
	Colm TRESSON	(Bray Wanderers AFC)	13
5)	Alex NESOVIC	(Finn Harps FC/Bohemian FC)	12

Premier Division Top-scorers 2001-2002

1)	Glen CROWE	(Bohemian FC)	21
2)	Jason BYRNE	(Bray Wanderers AFC)	14
	Sean FRANCIS	(Shamrock Rovers FC)	14
	Charles Mbabazi LIVINGSTONE	(St. Patrick's Athletic FC)	14
5)	Tony GRANT	(Shamrock Rovers FC)	13

Premier Division Top-scorers 2002-2003

1)	Glen CROWE	(Bohemian FC)	18
2)	John O'FLYNN	(Cork City FC)	14
3)	Jason BYRNE	(Bray Wanderers AFC)	12
4)	Noel HUNT	(Shamrock Rovers FC)	11

Premier Division Top-scorers 2003

1)	Jason BYRNE	(Shelbourne FC)	21
2)	Glen CROWE	(Bohemian FC)	19
3)	Tony BIRD	(St. Patrick's Athletic FC)	14
	Andrew MYLER	(Drogheda United FC)	14
	John O'FLYNN	(Cork City FC)	14

Premier Division Top-scorers 2004

1)	Jason BYRNE	(Shelbourne FC)	24
2)	Glen CROWE	(Bohemian FC)	17
3)	Daryl MURPHY	(Waterford United FC)	14
	Declan O'BRIEN	(Drogheda United FC)	14
5)	Kevin DOYLE	(Cork City FC)	12

NATIONAL LEAGUE OF IRELAND CHAMPIONSHIPS

Season	Winners	Pts	Runners-up	Pts	(Max)
1921-22	St. James's Gate	23	Bohemians	21	28
1922-23	Shamrock Rovers	39	Shelbourne	34	44
1923-24	Bohemians	32	Shelbourne	28	36
1924-25	Shamrock Rovers	31	Bohemians	28	36
1925-26	Shelbourne	31	Shamrock Rovers	29	36
1926-27	Shamrock Rovers	32	Shelbourne	29	36
1927-28	Bohemians	31	Shelbourne	28	36
1928-29	Shelbourne	33	Bohemians	32	36
1929-30	Bohemians	30	Shelbourne	29	36
1930-31	Shelbourne	31	Dundalk	28	44
1931-32	Shamrock Rovers	32	Cork	29	44
1932-33	Dundalk	29	Shamrock Rovers	24	36
1933-34	Bohemians	27	Cork	26	36
1934-35	Dolphin	28	St. James's Gate	27	36
1935-36	Bohemians	36	Dolphin	33	44
1936-37	Sligo Rovers	34	Dundalk	24	44
1937-38	Shamrock Rovers	32	Waterford	31	44
1938-39	Shamrock Rovers	36	Sligo Rovers	27	44
1939-40	St.James's Gate	36	Shamrock Rovers	30	44
1940-41	Cork United	30	Waterford	30	40

Cork United were awarded the Championship as Waterford were unable to compete in the play-off due to a dispute over payment to players.

Season	Winners	Pts	Runners-up	Pts	(Max)
1941-42	Cork United	30	Shamrock Rovers	28	36
1942-43	Cork United	27	Dundalk	26	36
1943-44	Shelbourne	21	Limerick	20	28
1944-45	Cork United	22	Limerick	17	28
1945-46	Cork United	21	Drumcondra	19	28
1946-47	Shelbourne	19	Drumcondra	18	28
1947-48	Drumcondra	18	Dundalk	17	28
1948-49	Drumcondra	29	Shelbourne	23	36
1949-50	Cork Athletic	25	Drumcondra	25	36

Season	Winners	Pts	Runners-up	Pts	(Max)
1950-51	Cork Athletic	26	Sligo Rovers	25	36
1951-52	St. Patrick's Athletic	34	Shelbourne	31	44
1952-53	Shelbourne	30	Drumcondra	29	44
1953-54	Shamrock Rovers	30	Evergreen United	28	44
1954-55	St Patrick's Athletic	36	Waterford	33	44
1955-56	St Patrick's Athletic	34	Shamrock Rovers	31	44
1956-57	Shamrock Rovers	36	Drumcondra	31	44
1957-58	Drumcondra	33	Shamrock Rovers	31	44
1958-59	Shamrock Rovers	34	Evergreen United	29	44
1959-60	Limerick	30	Cork Celtic	28	44
1960-61	Drumcondra	33	St Patrick's Athletic	32	44
1961-62	Shelbourne	35	Cork Celtic	35	44

Shelbourne beat Cork Celtic by 1-0 in a play-off at Dalymount Park.

Season	Winners	Pts	Runners-up	Pts	(Max)
1962-63	Dundalk	24	Waterford	23	36
1963-64	Shamrock Rovers	35	Dundalk	30	44
1964-65	Drumcondra	32	Shamrock Rovers	31	44
1965-66	Waterford	36	Shamrock Rovers	34	44
1966-67	Dundalk	34	Bohemians	27	44
1967-68	Waterford	34	Dundalk	30	44
1968-69	Waterford	36	Shamrock Rovers	31	44
1969-70	Waterford	38	Shamrock Rovers	36	52
1970-71	Cork Hibernians	35	Shamrock Rovers	35	52

Cork Hibernians beat Shamrock Rovers 3-1 in a play-off at Dalymount Park.

Season	Winners	Pts	Runners-up	Pts	(Max)
1971-72	Waterford	44	Cork Hibernians	40	52
1972-73	Waterford	42	Finn Harps	41	52
1973-74	Cork Celtic	42	Bohemians	38	52
1974-75	Bohemians	42	Athlone Town	33	52
1975-76	Dundalk	40	Finn Harps	36	52
1976-77	Sligo Rovers	39	Bohemians	38	52
1977-78	Bohemians	44	Finn Harps	42	60
1978-79	Dundalk	45	Bohemians	43	60
1979-80	Limerick United	47	Dundalk	46	60
1980-81	Athlone Town	51	Dundalk	45	60

Season	Winners	Pts	Runners-up	Pts	(Max)
1981-82	Dundalk	80	Shamrock Rovers	76	105
1982-83	Athlone Town	65	Drogheda United	49	78
1983-84	Shamrock Rovers	42	Bohemians	36	52
1984-85	Shamrock Rovers	49	Bohemians	43	60

NATIONAL LEAGUE OF IRELAND HISTORY
PREMIER DIVISION CHAMPIONSHIPS

Season	Winners	Pts	Runners-up	Pts	(Max)
1985-86	Shamrock Rovers	33	Galway United	31	44
1986-87	Shamrock Rovers	39	Dundalk	30	44
1987-88	Dundalk	46	St Patrick's Athletic	45	66
1988-89	Derry City	53	Dundalk	49	66
1989-90	St Patrick's Athletic	52	Derry City	49	66
1990-91	Dundalk	52	Cork City	50	66
1991-92	Shelbourne	49	Derry City	44	66
1992-93	Cork City	40	Bohemians	40	64

Three-way tie also involving Shelbourne. The teams played each other on a home and away basis and then on a on round league system at neutral venues.

Season	Winners	Pts	Runners-up	Pts	(Max)
1993-94	Shamrock Rovers	66	Cork City	59	96
1994-95	Dundalk	59	Derry City	58	99
1995-96	St Patrick's Athletic	67	Bohemians	62	99
1996-97	Derry City	67	Bohemians	57	99
1997-98	St Patrick's Athletic	68	Shelbourne	67	99
1998-99	St Patrick's Athletic	73	Cork City	70	99
1999-2000	Shelbourne	69	Cork City	58	99
2000-01	Bohemians	62	Shelbourne	60	99
2001-02	Shelbourne	63	Shamrock Rovers	57	99
2002-03	Bohemians	54	Shelbourne	49	81
2003	Shelbourne	69	Bohemians	64	108
2004	Shelbourne	68	Cork City	65	108

NATIONAL LEAGUE OF IRELAND HISTORY
FIRST DIVISION CHAMPIONSHIPS

Season	Winners	Pts	Runners-up	Pts	(Max)
1985-86	Bray Wanderers	28	Sligo Rovers	27	36
1986-87	Derry City	33	Shelbourne	27	36
1987-88	Athlone Town	39	Cobh Ramblers	38	54
1988-89	Drogheda United	39	University College Dublin	34	54
1989-90	Waterford United	37	Sligo Rovers	37	54

Waterford United beat Sligo Rovers 2-1 on aggregate in a play-off.

Season	Winners	Pts	Runners-up	Pts	(Max)
1990-91	Drogheda United	41	Bray Wanderers	38	54
1991-92	Limerick City	38	Waterford United	33	54
1992-93	Galway United	38	Cobh Ramblers	35	54
1993-94	Sligo Rovers	50	Athlone Town	46	81
1994-95	University College Dublin	64	Drogheda United	58	81
1995-96	Bray Wanderers	55	Finn Harps	49	81
1996-97	Kilkenny City	55	Drogheda United	44	81
1997-98	Waterford United	60	Bray Wanderers	54	81
1998-99	Drogheda United	64	Galway United	64	108

Drogheda United won the title on goal difference.

Season	Winners	Pts	Runners-up	Pts	(Max)
1999-2000	Bray Wanderers	72	Longford Town	70	108
2000-01	Dundalk	69	Monaghan United	65	108
2001-02	Drogheda United	58	Finn Harps	54	96
2002-03	Waterford United	46	Finn Harps	41	66
2003	Dublin City	67	Bray Wanderers	64	99
2004	Finn Harps	76	University College Dublin	75	99

FAI SENIOR CUP HISTORY

YEAR	WINNER	RUNNER-UP
1922	St. James's Gate	Shamrock Rovers
1923	Alton United	Shelbourne
1924	Athlone Town	Fordsons
1925	Shamrock Rovers	Shelbourne
1926	Fordsons	Shamrock Rovers
1927	Drumcondra	Brideville
1928	Bohemians	Drumcondra
1929	Shamrock Rovers	Bohemians
1930	Shamrock Rovers	Brideville
1931	Shamrock Rovers	Dundalk
1932	Shamrock Rovers	Dolphin
1933	Shamrock Rovers	Dolphin
1934	Cork	St. James's Gate
1935	Bohemians	Dundalk
1936	Shamrock Rovers	Cork
1937	Waterford	St. James's Gate
1938	St. James's Gate	Dundalk
1939	Shelbourne	Sligo Rovers
1940	Shamrock Rovers	Sligo Rovers
1941	Cork United	Waterford
1942	Dundalk	Cork United
1943	Drumcondra	Cork United
1944	Shamrock Rovers	Shelbourne
1945	Shamrock Rovers	Bohemians
1946	Drumcondra	Shamrock Rovers
1947	Cork United	Bohemians
1948	Shamrock Rovers	Drumcondra
1949	Dundalk	Shelbourne
1950	Transport	Cork Athletic
1951	Cork Athletic	Shelbourne
1952	Dundalk	Cork Athletic

Year	Winner	Runner-up
1953	Cork Athletic	Evergreen United
1954	Drumcondra	St. Patrick's Athletic
1955	Shamrock Rovers	Drumcondra
1956	Shamrock Rovers	Cork Athletic
1957	Drumcondra	Shamrock Rovers
1958	Dundalk	Shamrock Rovers
1959	St. Patrick's Athletic	Waterford
1960	Shelbourne	Cork Hibernians
1961	St. Patrick's Athletic	Drumcondra
1962	Shamrock Rovers	Shelbourne
1963	Shelbourne	Cork Hibernians
1964	Shamrock Rovers	Cork Celtic
1965	Shamrock Rovers	Limerick
1966	Shamrock Rovers	Limerick
1967	Shamrock Rovers	St. Patrick's Athletic
1968	Shamrock Rovers	Waterford
1969	Shamrock Rovers	Cork Celtic
1970	Bohemians	Sligo Rovers
1971	Limerick	Drogheda
1972	Cork Hibernians	Waterford
1973	Cork Hibernians	Shelbourne
1974	Finn Harps	St. Patrick's Athletic
1975	Home Farm	Shelbourne
1976	Bohemians	Drogheda
1977	Dundalk	Limerick
1978	Shamrock Rovers	Sligo Rovers
1979	Dundalk	Waterford
1980	Waterford	St. Patrick's Athletic
1981	Dundalk	Sligo Rovers
1982	Limerick United	Bohemians
1983	Sligo Rovers	Bohemians
1984	University College Dublin	Shamrock Rovers
1985	Shamrock Rovers	Galway United

Year	Winner	Runner-up
1986	Shamrock Rovers	Waterford United
1987	Shamrock Rovers	Dundalk
1988	Dundalk	Derry City
1989	Derry City	Cork City
1990	Bray Wanderers	St. Francis
1991	Galway United	Shamrock Rovers
1992	Bohemians	Cork City
1993	Shelbourne	Dundalk
1994	Sligo Rovers	Derry City
1995	Derry City	Shelbourne
1996	Shelbourne	St. Patrick's Athletic
1997	Shelbourne	Derry City
1998	Cork City	Shelbourne
1999	Bray Wanderers	Finn Harps
2000	Shelbourne	Bohemians
2001	Bohemians	Longford Town
2002	Dundalk	Bohemians
2002 (Interim season)	Derry City	Shamrock Rovers
2003	Longford Town	St. Patrick's Athletic
2004	Longford Town	Waterford United

EIRCOM LEAGUE CUP HISTORY

YEAR	WINNER	RUNNER-UP
1973/74	Waterford United	Finn Harps
1974/75	Bohemians	Finn Harps
1975/76	Limerick	Sligo Rovers
1976/77	Shamrock Rovers	Sligo Rovers
1977/78	Dundalk	Cork Alberts
1978/79	Bohemians	Shamrock Rovers
1979/80	Athlone Town	St. Patrick's Athletic
1980/81	Dundalk	Galway United
1981/82	Athlone Town	Shamrock Rovers
1982/83	Athlone Town	Dundalk
1983/84	Drogheda United	Athlone Town
1984/85	Waterford United	Finn Harps
1985/86	Galway United	Dundalk
1986/87	Dundalk	Shamrock Rovers
1987/88	Cork City	Shamrock Rovers
1988/89	Derry City	Dundalk
1989/90	Dundalk	Derry City
1990/91	Derry City	Limerick
1991/92	Derry City	Bohemians
1992/93	Limerick	St. Patrick's Athletic
1993/94	Derry City	Shelbourne
1994/95	Cork City	Dundalk
1995/96	Shelbourne	Sligo Rovers
1996/97	Galway United	Cork City
1997/98	Sligo Rovers	Shelbourne
1998/99	Cork City	Shamrock Rovers
1999/00	Derry City	Athlone Town
2000/01	St. Patrick's Athletic	University College Dublin
2001/02	Limerick	Derry City
2003	St. Patrick's Athletic	Longford Town
2004	Longford Town	Bohemians

Also available from Soccer Books Ltd. –

Alex Graham

A statistical record of football in the Republic of Ireland featuring every League result and Final League table, FAI Cup results from the Quarter-finals onwards and lists of top goalscorers. ISBN 1-86223-113-3.

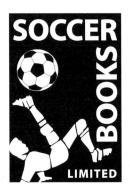

Softback Price £ 16.50   (€ 23.99)

Available from all good book shops or order direct –

Soccer Books Limited
72 St. Peters Avenue
Cleethorpes
DN35 8HU
United Kingdom

Web site– www.soccer-books.co.uk